What others are saying about the *Putting the "Happily" Into Your Ever After* marriage enrichment program

Marriage enrichment comes only through hard work and dedicated effort; however, having a marriage coach or mentor working with you as a couple allows you to *focus on what needs to be done and then do it!* Ed and Angie Wright's workbook-mentoring program is unexcelled and can transform a "so-so" or failing marriage into a dynamic interchange of two individuals whose marriage is not only enriched but thrives. It goes far beyond the "read my book" appeal of many authors but embraces an interaction between couples and mentors. I wholeheartedly endorse the book, *Putting the "Happily" Into Your Ever After*. It's a winner that will bring marital intimacy, communication, growth, and the blessing of God.

> **Harold J. Sala**, Ph.D., founder and president of *Guidelines International*

Ed and Angie Wright have a passion for marriages that is contagious. While their own marriage has not been perfect, it is a beautiful story of two people committed to God and each other. In *Putting the "Happily" Into Your Ever After* they offer some excellent insights on things that took their marriage from good to great. You will enjoy your journey with them.

> **Shannon Primicerio**, author, speaker & Bible study teacher

I enthusiastically recommend *Putting the "Happily" Into Your Ever After* and suggest that ALL couples use it—regardless of how long they have been married! Ed and Angie successfully cover the most important dynamics for all husbands and wives to know and practice. They have succinctly presented information that is crucial for marriages to become equipped with, and do it in a way that is interesting, easy to read and timeless in importance. This workbook will help marriages glorify God through their growth and obedience to the truths of God's Word, and just simply make being married more fulfilling fun the way God intended!

> **Scott Meacham**, M.A.B.S., M.A., PsyD (ABD), Licensed Minister/Certified Counselor

It's all too easy for a marriage counselor to sprinkle Scripture on secular philosophy or present ideas they've never actually lived. But I've observed Ed and Angie Wright's relationship and I'm impressed with their faithfulness to Scripture and the quality of their own marriage. They practice what they teach and it has given them a robust marriage from which they help other couples flourish.

> **Clay Jones**, D.Min., M.Div., Associate Professor of Christian Apologetics, Biola University

All of us want a marriage full of joy and peace. That is also God's plan for our marriage. We move towards that goal when we bring Him into the center of our marriage and use His Word to guide us. In *Putting the "Happily" Into Your Ever After*, Ed, Angie, and Kathy Jo have combined God's Word with real life examples and practical tips that will benefit all of our marriages. I enthusiastically recommend this workbook to any couple who wants to move towards a more God honoring marriage relationship.

Tom Atkins, Pastor to Couples and International Small Groups, Saddleback Church

Putting the "Happily" Into Your Ever After is a must have for all couples who are considering marriage or are already married. This workbook contains tools and guidance to set couples up for success and prevent divorce. I am excited to implement the workbook as part of our program at The Crossing and I urge other churches to do the same.

Randy Moraitis, MA, BCPC, Executive Pastor of Ministry at The Crossing Church, Board Certified Pastoral Counselor

PUTTING THE "Happily" INTO YOUR Ever After!

WORKBOOK

Ed & Angie Wright and Kathy Jo Stones, M.F.T.

MARRIAGE BY GOD is a ministry of Guidelines International Ministries,
Mission Viejo, California

Putting the "Happily" Into Your Ever After!
Copyright © 2012, 2015 by Ed Wright.

Request for information or comments should be emailed to Angie@MarriagebyGOD.org.

Unless otherwise indicated, all Scripture quotations are from the HOLY BIBLE, NEW INTERNATIONAL VERSION®, copyright © 1973, 1978, 1984 by International Bible Society.

Cover photography by Gavin Wade Photographers, Orange County, CA, http://gavinwadephoto.com.

Casey and Corey, you have made us laugh a lot and cry a little, but most of all you opened a chamber in our hearts we never knew existed. We could not love you more, or be more proud of you. May this book inspire you to love your wives with an outpouring of Christ's love, and may you receive God's richest blessings for your lives.
❧ Ed & Angie

To my husband and best friend Rich—your unconditional love, steadfast faith, and never-ending support and encouragement inspire my life daily.
❧ Kathy Jo

A special thanks to the many couples we have met through the years. It has been an honor and privilege to work with you.
❧ Ed, Angie & Kathy Jo

Contents

Introduction ix

Session I 1

    Taking an Inventory of Your Marriage 3

    Love Spoken Here 7

    The Freedom of Forgiveness 13

Session II 19

    Putting Christ at the Center of Your Marriage 21

    Developing an Intentional Marriage 31

    Finding the Sweet Spot in your Marriage 37

Session III 43

    Personality Differences 45

    Differences between Men and Women 49

    Love Languages 57

Session IV 63

    Family and Extended Family 65

    Communication 71

    Resolving Conflict 79

Session V 85

    Emotional Intimacy 87

    Physical Intimacy 93

Affair Proofing Your Marriage 101

Session VI 107

    Finances 109

    Marriage Goals 121

    Keeping the Flame Going... 129

Appendices 137

    What it Means to be a Submissive Wife 139

    What it Means to be a Godly Husband 141

    Guide to Planning a Date Night with Your Spouse 143

    The Five Love Languages Test for Wives...................................... 144

    The Five Love Languages Test for Husbands................................ 148

    Love Languages Guide 152

    Rules for Discussion 153

    Ten Rules to Resolve Conflict 154

    Ten Ways to be a Fantastic Wife.. 155

    Ten Ways to be a Fantastic Husband 156

        Acknowledgement 157

Introduction

IN 1999, AS OUR SONS WENT off to college and we became empty nesters, Ed announced that it was a good time for us to get involved in church ministry. This was amazing on so many levels. For many years, although Ed professed God as his Creator, and Jesus as his Savior, he had very little to show that he had wholeheartedly made Christ Lord of his life. I (Angie) had prayed for nearly eighteen years for Ed to take his role as the spiritual leader of our family more seriously. I had also prayed for him to be more understanding and supportive of my desire to be involved in Bible studies and women's ministry, for it seemed like my involvement caused more friction than spirituality in our relationship. By the time Ed made his announcement, I had given up dreaming that Ed would get involved in ministry, although I secretly mentioned to God a time or two that with all of Ed's gifts, if he ever *did* get involved, he was someone God could use mightily.

So I was shocked when Ed announced that day that we should explore ministries. But I shouldn't have been. Ed had been showing signs of spiritual growth by attending church more regularly and encouraging us to get baptized as a family. I had so resigned myself to the idea that Ed was not going to take his role as the spiritual leader more seriously that I was blind to how God had been working on his heart.

At that time we were attending Saddleback Church in Lake Forest, California, which was pastored by Dr. Rick Warren. Kathy Jo Stones, the new Director of Pastoral Care, had recently started a premarital counseling ministry. One of her biggest challenges was leading the church lay counseling ministry of over one hundred counselors. When she came on staff, lay counselors did the premarital counseling—one individual lay counselor working with each premarital couple. She tells the story:

> One day I sat in while one of the counselors counseled a premarital couple. Even though the counselor was astute and intuitive, he was not a married man, nor had he been trained in the specific issues related to premarital couples. After observing this dynamic, I envisioned the possibility of married couples counseling premarital couples. I imagined the married couple being trained specifically to work with premarital couples, establishing a mentoring relationship and using their years of marriage experience.

With her passion for building strong marriages, Kathy Jo masterfully crafted a unique premarital counseling program in which mature Christian married couples mentored engaged couples for six weeks. The ministry was an immediate success. An incredible number of married couples wanted to become premarital counselors!

We (Ed and Angie) thought it would be fun to engage in a ministry we could do together, so we attended one of the earliest training classes Kathy Jo taught. She had compiled materials from numerous resources. As great as the program was, the materials were a little cumbersome and confusing. They did not complement the outstanding program she had launched. Ed has great organizational and business skills, so a few months later, he approached Kathy Jo and offered our services to research and write material tailored to the program format. He envisioned making it concise and friendly, yet still comprehensive. We read, researched, and keenly observed everything we could for a year in order to produce the curriculum that Saddleback Church has used since 2002. That curriculum is now used by churches throughout the world.

We originally became involved in this ministry in an effort to give back to God, but we quickly learned we could not out give God. After just a short time in this ministry, God blessed our relationship and made our good marriage better than we ever dreamed possible. Counseling others on the principles of living a Christ-centered marriage blessed our marriage with a oneness we had never experienced before. Today, we have an amazing relationship. It is not perfect, but there are far more ups than downs. Even better, the ups are higher, and the downs, not so low. The downs get back on track within a few minutes or hours instead of days. We continue to grow every year in new and exciting ways.

And we are not alone. The other Marriage by God counselors experienced this same blessing in their own marriages.

Little did we know that the Premarital Counseling Ministry at Saddleback Church was going to be just the beginning of the journey on which God would take us. He showed us over and over again that we pray too small, and that God is much bigger than we believed.

God opened doors for our premarital program to spread abroad to the Philippines, China, India, Singapore, New Zealand, Argentina, and Russia. He provided opportunities for us to share our passion in all-day conferences in the Philippines and Singapore. Through some amazing circumstances, He even had us share Christian marriage principles with a secular audience at the TEDx talks in Albany, New York.

God also took Kathy Jo on an incredible journey. Her passion for counseling—especially couples—grew during her years at Saddleback. To continue developing her skills, she went back to school for a graduate degree in clinical psychology, with an emphasis in marriage and family therapy. In 2007, she received her Marriage and Family Therapist license. She currently has a thriving private practice in Mission Viejo. Working with couples is her passion and specialty.

Over the years, we kept in touch with Kathy Jo and her husband Rich. They have been blessed with a loving forty-year marriage. We all enjoyed discussing how God's plan and purpose for every marriage is more wonderful than most ever realize. As we shared our passionate convictions that God will show His power within our marriages if we submit to His plan and His leading, we began to feel God was guiding us to work together on a similar marriage enrichment program for couples. From this came *Putting the "Happily" Into Your Ever After*.

Working together on this project has been one of the greatest honors and privileges we have ever enjoyed! Throughout the material, Kathy Jo shares enlightening counseling experiences (of course, the names and some of the details are changed to protect identities). We share some of our real-life struggles and God's power to make things right. We also pass on some of the wonderful stories we've encountered during our twelve years of lay counseling.

What to Expect

This personalized curriculum guides you through sound biblical teachings, great discussions, challenging principles, and fun exercises. A Christian couple who has completed the program and received additional training will mentor you for six sessions. They are not professional counselors, nor do they have a perfect marriage. They do, however, possess numerous years of marriage experience, and they have encountered many of the same problems and issues you have in your marriage. They have a passion to live out a Christ-centered marriage and to help others navigate doing the same. They are involved in this ministry as a way to live out loving God and loving others. Your mentor couple's goal is not to solve problems for you, but to equip you with the tools necessary for you to solve your own problems. As the old saying goes, "Give a man a fish and you feed him for a day; teach a man to fish and you feed him for a lifetime."

As you start the workbook, please remember that the more honest and open you are with your answers, the more you will get out of the program. The effort you put into this program will come back to you exponentially!

Please complete each session's lessons before you meet. Please complete the workbook separately from your spouse, and do not discuss the chapter or answers with anyone prior to your session.

Here are a few suggestions that will make your experience more enjoyable and profitable:

o   Arrive on time.
o   Go into your sessions with an open and positive mind.
o   Come prepared to meet for approximately two hours.

Studies show that the happiest people in the world are married, but sadly, the unhappiest people in the world are also married. The goal of this program is to take you on a journey to become one of the happiest couples. As you can see, the stakes are high and the goal is lofty, but we want you to understand what it is to put the "happily" into your ever after!

Session I

Chapter 1 ❧ Taking an Inventory of Your Marriage

Chapter 2 ❧ Love Spoken Here

Chapter 3 ❧ The Freedom of Forgiveness

CHAPTER 1

Taking an Inventory of Your Marriage

For this reason a man will leave his father and
mother and be united to his wife, and they will
become one flesh—Genesis 2:24

IN 1978 ANGIE AND I (Ed) blissfully walked down the aisle
to begin our "happily ever after." Angie was just nineteen years
old and I was twenty-six. Although we would both have called
ourselves Christians—we both acknowledged God as our
Creator and Christ as our Savior—neither one of us really knew
what it was to fully surrender and make God Lord of our lives.
We both felt committed to living good moral lives to the best
of our abilities. Angie felt compelled to follow the "good
Christian way" of going to church every Sunday. I felt that
since I had to work many weekends, she could cover the
spiritual base for our family most of the time.

We settled into marriage. A few years later we started our
family. Our oldest son, Casey, arrived in 1981 followed by his
younger brother, Corey, just thirteen months later. Instead of
going back to work full-time after our second son was born,
Angie worked alongside me in our real estate business. As the
stresses of family and work mounted, so did the strain in our
relationship. We learned to make things work, but it seemed as
if we were more like great roommates than husband and wife.
Things weren't horrible: they were just a lot less than either one
of us had expected in our marriage.

Before we married, we went through premarital counseling
classes taught by an unmarried pastor to a classroom full of

engaged couples. We learned a few things, but were not really equipped with effective tools to draw on as we entered our marriage. Most marriages go from "I do" to "What do I do now?" That was we. We were still very much in love, but we had no idea how to live the married life about which we had both dreamed.

If you identify with some of this, then this program is for you. We are going take you on a journey to acquire some wonderful tools to live out God's design for marriage.

Let's get started with some foundational concepts.

From the very beginning God wanted a husband and wife to operate together as a singular unit. Genesis 2:24 states, "For this reason a man will leave his father and mother and be *united* to his wife, and they will become *one flesh*" (emphasis added). The Hebrew word used for *united*, *dabaq*, means "to cling, cleave, keep close, stick to, or adhere to" (like glue). So we can think of marriage as being "glued together into one flesh." And as Jesus firmly states, "Therefore what God has joined together, let man not separate" (Mark 10:9). That sounds pretty permanent!

In order for a husband and wife to truly stick together as one flesh the way God intends, they have to submit to the leading of the Holy Spirit in their relationship. The Holy Spirit is the glue that unites them together as one. If this is difficult to comprehend, it is with good reason: "'For this reason a man will leave his father and mother and be united to his wife, and the two will become one flesh.' *This is a profound mystery*" (Ephesians 5:31–32, emphasis added). God intends for the husband and wife relationship to be uniquely united in a oneness unlike any other earthly relationship. This is a mystery that can only be accomplished when God binds together a couple submitted to the Holy Spirit.

One of the foundational ideas that differentiate a secular marriage from a God-centered marriage is that a God-centered marriage assumes a union of three: God, husband, and wife. Ecclesiastes 4:12 says, "Though one may be overpowered, two can defend themselves. A cord of three strands is not quickly broken." A cord or braid appears to contain only two strands, but it is impossible to create a braid with only two strands. If just two strands are wrapped together, they quickly unravel. Herein lies the mystery: What looks like two strands requires a

God intends for the husband and wife relationship to be uniquely united in a oneness unlike any other earthly relationship

third. The third strand, though not immediately visible keeps the strands tightly woven.

In a Christian marriage, God's presence, like that third strand in a braid, holds the husband and wife together. As a couple, one of the most important steps towards creating a strong marriage is placing God as the leader. We submit to God being Lord of our lives and Lord of our marriage. In a practical way, we acknowledge the need to have God in control of all of our decisions, directing and leading every aspect of our lives.

Please answer all of the following questions independently of your spouse. Do not compare answers until you meet with your mentors.

1. **On a scale of 1 to 10 (10 being best), how would you rate your marriage?**

2. **Are you putting as much effort into your marriage as you did during your courtship?**

3. **What would you like to see God accomplish through this mentoring program? Be specific.**

4. How do you feel about divorce?

5. On a scale of 1 to 10, rate your compatibility in the
    seven areas below.

    1 = not compatible at all
    10 = extremely compatible

Factor	Rating
Fun	
Friendship	
Finance	
Family	
Forgiveness	
Future	
Faith	

CHAPTER 2

Love Spoken Here

God is love—1 John 4:8

WE WILL NEVER FORGET A discussion many years ago at a dinner with two other married couples. Ed shared about a study he had read that concluded if you kiss your wife goodbye every morning and tell her you love her, you will not only have a better marriage, you will live five years longer and make 20 percent more income than those who do not. Whether or not the study actually had merit, it certainly led to some lively discussion that evening. I (Angie) started off by saying that Ed is very good about kissing me goodbye every morning, even when he is leaving at 5:30 a.m. to play basketball. I also said that he is the *best* at saying "I love you" to me throughout the day. Then Karen said that her husband Dan was also great about kissing her goodbye and telling her often that he loves her. At this point Lisa sadly turned to her husband, Rob, and said, "Rob, you never tell me you love me." Rob looked at Lisa and said, "I told you I loved you before we got married. If I ever change my mind, I will let you know." We all laughed— all of us, except for Lisa. Rob's failure to communicate his love to Lisa had clearly caused deep hurt.

That simple little word *love* so profoundly impacts a marriage that it needs to be communicated in words and actions daily.

When the two of you came together on your wedding day, your family and friends could easily see that you were in love. However, *love* is hard to define, perhaps because there are so many types of love but just one English word to describe them. We say we love our spouse, we love our children, we love our car, and we love ice cream. We use the same word "love" in all of these examples, though with very different meanings. To help us differentiate, we'll use three words the ancient Greeks used for love: *eros*, *philia*, and *agape*.

Eros is romantic, sensual, or sexual love. In a sexually fulfilling marriage, a husband and wife will be physically attracted to one another and love each other romantically. Eros is the root of the word *erotic*, which means "to arouse sexual desire or excitement."

Philia is friendship love. Friendship means companionship, communication, and cooperation. This is the type of love we have for friends. Philadelphia, the city of brotherly love, takes its name from this word. Spouses should be each other's best friend.

Agape is totally committed love. God's love for us is agape love. His love is sacrificial, unconditional, forgiving, and eternal. In marriage, agape love is not something that just happens. It requires full commitment to wanting only the best for your spouse. Agape love keeps on giving—it is completely selfless. This kind of love is not just a feeling, but an act of the will. Agape love in marriage tells us to deny ourselves and to put our spouse first.

The goal for a fulfilling marriage is to keep all three types of love strong. The oneness that God designed for couples to experience is a product of eros, philia, and agape love working together continuously in the relationship.

In coming chapters, we will look closely at eros and philia love. In this chapter, we will examine how agape love is expressed in marriage. We will also see how God's agape love is a model of how we should love God, our spouse, and others.

Agape love, or selfless love, usually runs contrary to our selfish, sinful nature. In our marriage and in other relationships, we want our own needs met. We want to feel good about ourselves and protect our rights. This is contrary to God's ways. He wants us to put ourselves aside and place Him (God) first, and others second. When asked which commandment was greatest, Jesus said, "'Love the Lord your God with all your heart and with all your soul and with all your mind and with all your strength.' The second is this: 'Love your neighbor as yourself.' There is no commandment greater than

If you look at your spouse through God's eyes, you will see him or her differently

these" (Mark 12:30–31). When we follow this command and love others in this way, we glorify God.

To love others, we need to first receive and experience God's love ourselves. Knowing how much God loves us allows us to love others more fully. First John 4:7–8 says, "Dear friends, let us love one another, for love comes from God. Everyone who loves has been born of God and knows God. Whoever does not love does not know God, because *God is love*" (emphasis added). God *is* love! Love is not just an emotion that God created, but it is the full embodiment of God Himself! As you meditate on God's love for you, begin to reflect on His love for your spouse. If you look at your spouse through God's eyes, you will see him or her differently.

If love in your marriage is missing or strained, go to love's source: God. Talk to Him in prayer and read His love letter to you. The Old Testament tells the story of God's faithful love for Israel even when they rejected or abandoned Him. Isaiah 43:25 says, "I, even I, am he who blots out your transgressions, for my own sake, and remembers your sins no more." This is the love God has for us and wants us to have towards our spouse. First Peter 4:8 says, "Above all, love each other deeply, because love covers over a multitude of sins." God sees us fail repeatedly, yet He is never impatient or unkind. God sees our wrongdoings, but He doesn't record them. His love is long-suffering and His forgiveness is never ending. God never gives up on us, and He wants us to love our spouse in the same way.

God never gives up on us, and He wants us to love our spouse in the same way

Remember, agape is not a feeling, but an act of the will. Choose to act lovingly, in obedience to God's commands, even if you do not *feel* loving towards your spouse. Romans 5:3–5 says, "We also rejoice in our sufferings, because we know that suffering produces perseverance; perseverance, character; and character, hope. And hope does not disappoint us, because *God has poured out his love into our hearts by the Holy Spirit, whom he has given us*" (emphasis added). When you struggle with loving your spouse, ask God to fill you with His love towards your spouse. Even if your spouse does not respond to your love, you will draw into a more intimate relationship with God through your obedience.

One Saturday night, I (Angie) sat in church mad at Ed over an argument that had left me angry and hurt. At that time, my way of dealing with hurt was withdrawal, and I was on day two of giving Ed the cold shoulder and silent treatment. Author Lee

Strobel (*The Case for Christ*) was the guest speaker and it happened to be his twentieth wedding anniversary. So as I sat there stewing, he began talking about love and marriage. Not exactly what I wanted to hear. He shared that for their anniversary he was giving his wife a Letterman-style Top Ten List of the ten things he loved most about her. As I sat there, I began to think of all the things I loved about Ed. I easily reached ten. As I did, God began to soften my heart. The hurt and anger dissipated. I then began to think, I bet I could come up with 100 things I love about Ed. Over the next few days, I kept adding to my list. By the end of the week I presented it to Ed. When he began reading it, he gave me a big grin. As he continued, his face softened. When he finished, my big strong husband had a tear softly running down his cheek. He was truly touched.

I learned a valuable lesson that night. Our emotions reflect what we choose to focus on. When I focused on my own hurt, I felt hurt and angry. When I focused on my love for Ed, I was filled with the love of God. I vowed that day to choose to focus on loving others, especially Ed, rather than concentrating on my self-centered, unmet expectations.

Our emotions reflect what we choose to focus on

During the next year, Ed gave me a similar list, we gave our sons lists, and they gave us lists. Over the years we have shared this story with others who have created lists for loved ones and received amazing results. They are a powerful way to express your love. They are also good to refer back to when you start to lose those loving feelings.

Another way to rekindle love in marriage is to reflect on when, how, where, and why you first fell in love with your spouse. If possible, reenact an early dating experience. Reminisce about the first time each of you told the other that you loved them. Put the same time, focus, and attention into your marriage as you did in the beginning of your relationship.

Agape love is different than the kinds of love the world offers. Worldly love suggests each spouse give 50/50. In other words, love equally—give only as much love as you receive. Agape love says give 100 percent. God desires both husband and wife to give 100 percent. Yet we have seen cases in which one spouse fully committed to God's agape love was enough to turn the relationship around.

God beautifully illustrates His love and gives us a model for how we should love our spouse:

Love is patient, love is kind. It does not envy, it does not boast, it is not proud. It is not rude, it is not self-seeking, it is not easily angered, it keeps no record of wrongs. Love does not delight in evil but rejoices with the truth. It always protects, always trusts, always hopes, always perseveres. Love never fails.

—1 Corinthians 13:4–8

God's love *never* fails! Is this the kind of unconditional love you have for your spouse?

I regularly ask myself, "What is the most loving thing I can do towards my spouse at this moment?" Sometimes it might just be to simply say, "I love you." Another time it might be to do something extra helpful. Still another time, it might be to give him a ten-minute foot massage (even if I am exhausted). Love comes in a lot of forms: words, thoughts, and actions. But love needs to be expressed daily through words and actions to be felt.

God shows us how to love sacrificially through agape love. He wants us to put aside our selfish ways and put others first. When we are in a relationship with God, our goal is to glorify Him through our actions, thoughts, and words. Loving our spouse with agape is one way that we demonstrate our obedience to His Word. Agape love brings glory to God. May you experience God's agape love in greater ways than ever before!

Please answer the following questions independently of your spouse. Do not compare your answers until our next session.

1. **Which of the three types of love needs the most growth in your marriage (eros, philia, or agape)?**

2. **How often does your spouse tell you that he or she loves you?**

3. If you were having a bad day, how could you avoid
    taking it out on your spouse?

4. Review the passage on love in 1 Corinthians 13:4–8.
    Which part of the love described is the most
    challenging for you to show your spouse? Why?

5. List ten things you love about your spouse.

CHAPTER 3

The Freedom of Forgiveness

Forgive as the Lord forgave you—Colossians 3:13

WE (ED AND ANGIE) WERE out to dinner with some friends. During the evening I thoughtlessly criticized Ed in a hurtful way. Not my proudest moment. As we got into the car to drive home, he expressed his disappointment. I told him I was sorry. He finished by saying, "I am going to be mad at you for three more minutes." We both started laughing. Ed had masterfully pointed out that I had wronged him, but kept the exchange about the hurtful situation light.

Forgiveness is important—especially within the context of marriage. All our spouses have wronged us, whether overtly or through omission. Sometimes these hurts are small and easily forgiven, while other wrongs leave us feeling devastated, wondering if we will ever recover. A marriage without forgiveness develops bitterness. Our inability to extend forgiveness will ultimately hurt us more than the person we are trying to hurt. Clinging to unforgiveness is like taking poison, thinking it will hurt the other person. Understanding and accepting God's love and forgiveness for us enables us to love and forgive our spouse. God's forgiveness, lovingly expressed within marriage, can bless the couple with a stronger, healthier relationship. In this chapter, we will explore the biblical model of forgiveness, how to process through the bigger hurts, and how to move quickly through little hurts.

God has given us the ultimate model of forgiveness in His agape (unconditional) love through the sacrificial gift of His Son, Jesus Christ. The gift of salvation is by grace, not because we earned or deserved it. Jesus commands us to forgive others because God has forgiven us. We must extend grace and forgiveness to our spouse, whether the offense is big or small, regardless of whether or not they repent.

God understands that forgiveness does not come naturally to us; nonetheless, He does not look lightly on unforgiveness. In Matthew 6:14–15, Jesus warns, "For if you forgive men when they sin against you, your heavenly Father will also forgive you. But if you do not forgive men their sins, your Father will not forgive your sins."

A group of Amish families demonstrated their deep understanding of this teaching. On October 2, 2006, gunman Charles Roberts took children hostage in an Amish school-house. He shot ten girls aged six to thirteen before turning the gun on himself. Five of the girls died. In a powerful expression of forgiveness, the Amish families who had buried their daughters the day before attended the killer's burial service and hugged the widow and other members of the killer's family. Later, they even donated money to the widow.

Forgiveness is first between God and us. God commands us to forgive even when we have done nothing to deserve the wrong that was done to us. C. S. Lewis refers to pain as the megaphone God uses to get our attention.[1] Sometimes there is a lesson that God is trying to teach us through our circumstances. God may be working on different lessons in you and your spouse through the same hurtful circumstance. Perhaps this poem sums it up best:

> People are often unreasonable, illogical, and self-centered. Forgive them anyway.
> …
> Give the world the best you have, and it may never be enough; give the world the best you've got anyway.
> You see, in the final analysis, it is between you and God; it was never between you and them anyway."[2]

Janet shed tears in my (Kathy Jo's) office as she described the shock of finding her husband, Peter, viewing pornography late one evening. Fortunately, he owned up to the truth. Peter knew his actions displeased God and that the resulting guilt and shame affected his desire to be close to his wife. When

Clinging to unforgiveness is like taking poison, thinking it will hurt the other person

---

[1] C. S. Lewis, *The Problem of Pain* (New York: Macmillan, 1962), 93.

[2] This poem is a modified version of "The Paradoxical Commandments of Leadership" by Kent M. Keith. http://quoteinvestigator.com/2012/05/18/do-good-anyway/#more-3828 (accessed 1/8/2015).

Janet discovered Peter's secret life, the pain seemed almost unbearable. How could she ever enjoy having sex without feeling hurt and betrayed? How could she trust that he didn't have other secrets? Peter realized that it would take a long time, with consistent accountability, to restore his wife's respect and trust. Janet knew she had to obey God and forgive Peter, but that the journey toward healing and forgiveness would be difficult.

Struggling to forgive is not sin. Choosing to harbor unforgiveness is. As we endeavor to forgive, we'll process anger, sadness, and loss. It will likely take a great deal of time and effort to experience the many feelings associated with a betrayal or breach of trust. Neglecting or minimizing healing steps may cause a couple to miss the lessons God wants to teach them to make their marriage better.

Perhaps the most disheartening situation requiring forgiveness is when the offense keeps recurring and there is no remorse or repentance. We need to forgive intentional, unrepentant offenses too.

God calls us to forgive those who have wronged us, but this does not mean that we must trust them. Mark 11:25 says, "And when you stand praying, if you hold anything against anyone, forgive him, so that your Father in heaven may forgive you your sins." Forgiveness and trust are two separate acts. Breached trust takes time to restore. Trust is earned back through consistent accountability over time. In Genesis 37–50, Joseph forgave his brothers for selling him into slavery. He recognized that what they had intended for evil, God had used for good. But when his brothers came back into his life, Joseph tested his brothers before trusting them.

Forgiveness and trust are two separate acts

If you are in the process of rebuilding trust towards your spouse, be patient and focus positively on their changed behavior. If your spouse is not willing to change behavior in order to rebuild trust, you may need to put boundaries in place to protect against future wrongs.

If you are the one who broke trust in the relationship, go out of your way to assure your spouse that your behavior has truly changed. Be accountable.

It is our prayer that you will never have to experience a big wound in your marriage; however, there are times in every marriage when small offenses happen. Perhaps your spouse forgot a promise or was late for an important event. Maybe your husband or wife forgot your birthday or wedding anniversary. You may be hurt by words that felt harsh. God wants us to offer forgiveness to our spouses freely, and apologize when we have done something wrong, without expecting anything in return. In Matthew 18:21–22, "Peter came to Jesus and asked, 'Lord, how many times shall I forgive my brother when he sins against me? Up to seven times?' Jesus answered, 'I tell you, not seven times, but seventy-seven times.'" Jesus knew that we would need to forgive others, especially our spouse, over and over again. With practice, this will become easier and more natural. Here are some thoughts to help cultivate a forgiving heart:

- We tend to judge others by their worst act and yet judge ourselves by our best intentions. We are usually quick to forgive ourselves and move past our shortcomings. We should give our spouse the same grace. Jesus said, "Why do you look at the speck of sawdust in your brother's eye and pay no attention to the plank in your own eye? ... You hypocrite, first take the plank out of your own eye, and then you will see clearly to remove the speck from your brother's eye" (Matthew 7:3, 5).

- Sometimes what we perceive as mean-spirited is merely misconstrued, mistakenly personalized, or misunderstood. Lovingly communicate your hurt feelings to your spouse and allow him or her to clarify. Then release your hurt to God. Honestly addressing your frustrations allows for understanding, whereas passivity usually causes frustrations to become pent-up and acted out in negative ways.

- Try to understand the motivation behind what was done to hurt you. It has been said, "Hurt people often hurt people." Perhaps your spouse did not deal with a given situation appropriately because he or she was hurting or insecure.

- When your spouse has wronged you, it is always good to put it into perspective. Reflect on your spouse's positive attributes. If you need help remembering, refer back to your list of ten things you love about your spouse (page 12).

- When we don't forgive our spouse, we allow negative thoughts to rent space in our mind.

- We will never have to forgive our spouse as much as God has forgiven us.

- It is good to remember that, at some time, we will also need forgiveness. Quite often, the very thing that we have trouble forgiving our spouse for is the same thing we will turn around and do to our spouse in a slightly different way. For instance, you may feel that your spouse is being critical of you in a certain area of your life; however, as you pay closer attention to what you say and do, you realize that you, too, are being critical towards your spouse in other areas.

- When something hurtful is said to you, there is often a grain of truth in it. Be open to examining your spouse's words and consider how you might make some positive changes. Accept the lesson and release the hurt.

- Make a commitment to each other that you will never go to bed without forgiving one another even if you have to finish the discussion later.

We'll need to forgive in many ways, many times, throughout our marriage. God's command to forgive will take an act of the will and may or may not involve a repentant, remorseful spouse. Forgiveness may also involve a process of healing and restoration. Satan would like to keep us in a state of unforgiveness. Don't give him that pleasure! When you struggle with forgiving your spouse, go to the source of love and forgiveness—God. And remember, "the one who is in you is greater than the one who is in the world" (1 John 4:4).

Please answer the following questions independently of your spouse. Do not compare your answers until our next session.

1. **Why is it important to forgive your spouse?**

2. When you forgive someone, must you also trust them?

3. Is there something for which you need to forgive your spouse? What is preventing you from extending forgiveness to him or her?

4. Is there anything for which you feel your spouse has never completely forgiven you?

Session II

Chapter 4 ❧ Putting Christ at the Center of Your Marriage

Chapter 5 ❧ Developing an Intentional Marriage

Chapter 6 ❧ Finding the Sweet Spot in your Marriage

CHAPTER 4

Putting Christ at the Center of Your Marriage

Jesus answered, "I am the way and the truth and the life. No one comes to the Father except through me."—John 14:6

FOR MORE YEARS THAN WE (Ed and Angie) would like to admit, we pursued our relationships with Christ individually, not as a couple. We went to church together, but we prayed, studied our Bibles, attended small group, and ministered separately. When we finally started attending small group Bible studies together, talking about God's will for our lives and marriage, and especially praying together regularly, we grew deeper in oneness than ever before. We came to realize there is a big difference between putting Christ at the center of your individual life and putting Christ at the center of your marriage.

We believe there are many Christian couples like us out there. They both believe in God and regularly attend church together, but they are afraid to get truly vulnerable with their spouse in prayer or to deeply discuss matters of faith together.

The Bible (1 Corinthians 11:3 and Ephesians 5:23) tells us that the husband is responsible for being the spiritual leader of the family. Although I (Ed) was successful in business and could speak at seminars to hundreds of people, I felt insecure about praying out loud with Angie. As I grew in my knowledge and understanding of God's Word, I came to understand the responsibility I was given as head of the house and began bringing the family together in prayer. I started small at first, gathering the whole family to pray together before we went to church each Sunday. After I got comfortable with that, I began praying more often at regularly scheduled times and spontaneously when special prayers were needed. Finally, Angie and I started praying together, just the two of us, in an open, deep, and vulnerable way.

One day Angie said, "Most people view the act of sex as being the most intimate expression of love and oneness in marriage. I disagree. The most intimate act a couple can do is to pray together. In sex you bare your bodies, but in prayer, you bare your souls." She was right. Today I understand that transparently praying together brings God into the oneness of a marriage. It puts you in tune with the leading of the Holy Spirit. When I decided to take my responsibility as spiritual leader seriously, the intimacy in our relationship intensified, and I modeled what it is to be a godly man to our sons.

This is not unique to us. A few years ago, we were training a group of couples to become premarital counselors. I posed a question to the group: "What does it mean to you when you pray together as a couple?" I was taken back when there was an audible sigh from the ladies. Shelia, one of our trainees, shared that as Frank and she crawl into bed at the end of the day, he almost always asks about her day. Then he prays for her. She said, "It is *so* romantic. It melts my heart." Then Frank piped in, "It's the best foreplay ever!"

Dr. Sala says, "It's a fact, according to valid research: The greater a couple's spiritual commitment, the more satisfying their sexual relationship."[3] Another special gift from God!

Let me share some of the guides I have used to lead my family in prayer. When we pray, we use simple, everyday language. We talk with God as though He were the third party in our conversation, sometimes even visualizing His presence by putting an empty chair in the room. In our conversation with God:

- **We give Him *praise*.** The Bible tells us that God created all things for His glory. Psalm 150:6 says, "Let everything that has breath praise the LORD. Praise the LORD." Our praise brings God great pleasure.

There is a big difference between putting Christ at the center of your individual life and putting Christ at the center of your marriage

[3] Harold J. Sala, "Prayer Therapy and Marriage," email to Guidelines Daily E-Commentary mailing list, February 21, 2007.

- **We give Him our *requests*.** Prayer is powerful. Jesus tells us in John 15:7, "If you remain in me and my words remain in you, ask whatever you wish, and it will be given you." The Apostle John confirmed Jesus' words with this assurance in 1 John 5:14–15: "This is the confidence we have in approaching God: that if we ask anything according to his will, he hears us. And if we know that he hears us—whatever we ask—we know that we have what we asked of him."

- **We give Him our *thanksgiving*.** In God's currency, asking and thanking are closely related. Philippians 4:6 says, "Do not be anxious about anything, but in everything, by prayer and petition, with thanksgiving, present your requests to God." We should cultivate a grateful heart and thankful attitude toward God. We can begin thanking Him before we even receive His response. We have been amazed at God's answered prayers when our hearts were right towards Him.

- **We give Him our *contrite hearts*.** Although all of our sins are forgiven through what Christ did for us on the Cross, God still wants us to come before Him and repent with a contrite, broken heart. God wants us to turn away from our sinful behavior. We regularly pray for God to reveal any sin in our lives.

Transparently praying together brings God into the oneness of a marriage

Several years ago we started an annual tradition of each of us writing out a prayer for our marriage on New Year's Day and sealing it in an envelope. Then the next New Year's Eve, we would open our prayers and read them to each other. The first year we did this, I (Angie) wrote a very safe, conservative prayer. God answered every word of it. Ed, on the other hand, wrote a big, bold prayer. We were blessed to see that God answered all of his prayer too. From that time on, we both have made it a practice to pray boldly in God's will. After all, the Bible says, "You do not have, because you do not ask God" (James 4:2).

Just as prayer unites us in marriage, it is also important to understand the unique roles God defined for husbands and wives, and how they were meant to strengthen the union. The Bible says that God first created Adam from the earth. Then He created Eve from Adam. Woman's purpose is found in Genesis 2:18: "The LORD God said, 'It is not good for the man to be alone. I will make a helper suitable for him.'" God created

Eve to be Adam's helpmate. God wants husbands and wives to work together as a team. In marriage, you are no longer two people who walk separately, concerned with getting your own way, but rather, two people who walk together in agape love as a team. Whereas in other parts of your life you may be placed to serve together with others, within your marriage, you are the only person who will have the role of husband or wife to your spouse. It is a unique position that God prepared for you alone!

The Apostle Paul further defined the roles of husbands and wives when he wrote, "For the husband is the head of the wife as Christ is the head of the church" (Ephesians 5:23). Paul speaks of this hierarchical chain of responsibility in this passage too: "Now I want you to realize that the head of every man is Christ, and the head of the woman is man, and the head of Christ is God" (1 Corinthians 11:3). This chain of responsibility may seem difficult to understand, yet we see it every day in the workplace: most of us are accountable to a boss, and even CEOs are usually accountable to a Board of Directors and stockholders.

A husband is accountable to God for how he loves his wife, regardless of whether she respects and submits to him

The role of the husband being the head of the wife in no way lessens her value. The Apostle Paul clarified this when he wrote, "There is neither Jew nor Greek, slave nor free, male nor female, for you are all one in Christ Jesus " (Galatians 3:28). Paul says that men and women enjoy equal status and privilege before God because of their position in Christ. However, equal status and marital roles are two different things.

The Holy Trinity (Father, Son, and Holy Spirit) is the perfect model for the way we should pattern ourselves in marriage. In her book, *The Excellent Wife,* Martha Peace explains it like this:

> The Trinity is a relationship in which three eternal persons (each perfect and totally equal in being, power, and glory) reveal, know, and love each other tenderly and perfectly for the other's good. When they decide to set and accomplish a goal, God the Son and God the Holy Spirit, although equal, voluntarily subordinate themselves to God the Father in order to accomplish their perfect plans. As they work together, they are totally unified in desire, thought, and action until the goal's completion. Thus they are a plurality within a unity.[4]

---

[4] Martha Peace, *The Excellent Wife* (Bemidji, MN: Focus Publications, 1997), 30.

The Trinity operates as one with different roles. Here is how God instructs husbands and wives to do the same in a Christian marriage:

> Submit to one another out of reverence for Christ.
>
> Wives, submit to your husbands as to the Lord. For the husband is the head of the wife as Christ is the head of the church, his body, of which he is the Savior. Now as the church submits to Christ, so also wives should submit to their husbands in everything.
>
> Husbands, love your wives, just as Christ loved the church and gave himself up for her to make her holy, cleansing her by the washing with water through the word, and to present her to himself as a radiant church, without stain or wrinkle or any other blemish, but holy and blameless. In this same way, husbands ought to love their wives as their own bodies. He who loves his wife loves himself. After all, no one ever hated his own body, but he feeds and cares for it, just as Christ does the church—for we are members of his body. "For this reason a man will leave his father and mother and be united to his wife, and the two will become one flesh." This is a profound mystery—but I am talking about Christ and the church. However, *each one of you also must love his wife as he loves himself, and the wife must respect her husband.*

> —Ephesians 5:21–33 (emphasis added)

This is God's desire and design for us in marriage. When the dynamics between a husband and wife are correct, their positive interactions will reflect honoring, praising, serving, loving, caring, trusting, and respecting one another. When the dynamics are incorrect, their negative interactions will reflect criticizing, nagging, complaining, blaming, and controlling. How well does your marriage reflect God's design?

The roles of husbands and wives are not conditional. A husband is accountable to God for how he loves his wife, regardless of whether she respects and submits to him. Conversely, a wife answers to God for how she submits to and respects her husband regardless of whether she agrees with his decisions or actions.

When God is at the center of our relationship, instead of just relying on our own strength, we are able to allow the Holy Spirit to work in and through us. This is why regularly coming together in prayer individually and as a couple is so important.

A wife answers to God for how she submits to and respects her husband regardless of whether she agrees with his decisions or actions

In addition to prayer, here are some additional ways to keep Christ at the center of your marriage:

- **Join a couples' small-group Bible study.**
- **Get involved in a ministry.** God has given you and your spouse a combination of opportunities and spiritual gifts that are uniquely designed for you. First Peter 4:10 states, "Each one should use whatever gift he has received to serve others, faithfully administering God's grace in its various forms." Pray and watch for God's leading in this area. He will place in your heart the direction He wants you to take. Consider whether there might be an area of ministry where your gifts would complement one another and you could serve together as a couple. You'll be blessed if you live in God's will with your time, treasure, and talents. (If you find that you are overstressed with any of these, you are likely not in God's will.) When you are living out God's will for your life, two things will result: you will be blessed to be a blessing, and you will not be able to out-give God!
- **Remove any idols from your life.** Removing idols may seem like an odd concept, but God wants us to love Him with all of our heart, mind, and soul. Anything we put above God in our lives is an idol. Idols are what we worship and trust in. We need to become more aware of what's on our mind, what we long for, what is really important to us, and what we have our heart set on. It's common for jobs or ministry to become idols. Ironically, we can even make our spouses (or kids) idols in our lives because we are so intent on pleasing them. God should be our greatest longing and desire. Our thoughts, motives, and choices should be set on glorifying Him.
- **Be intentional about seeking God's will in every situation, big or small.** In order to follow God's will we need to first know His will. Romans 12:2 says, "Do not conform any longer to the pattern of this world, but be transformed by the renewing of your mind. Then you will be able to test and approve what God's will is—his good, pleasing and perfect will." We can renew our minds through reading the Bible, praying, and seeking godly counsel from other mature Christians, but even then our selfish desires and sinful responses keep us from staying in tune with God. We need to continually refocus our living

day-by-day, walking step-by-step in His will through the guidance of the Holy Spirit.

This entire program is focused on putting Christ at the center of our marriages. Prayer is the greatest means for accomplishing this. Prayer acknowledges God's presence and softens our hearts towards one another. It is the perfect pathway to calm emotions when strife arises. It helps our wills conform to the roles God has given us in marriage. It releases the power of the Holy Spirit to help and guide us. When we share our deepest thoughts and emotions with our spouse openly and honestly in prayer, we are able to emotionally unite in body, soul, and spirit the way God intended us to in marriage.

God wants to be at the center of our marriages in every way. When a couple makes Christ Lord of all areas of their marriage, they truly do become one in Christ!

Please answer the following questions independently of your spouse. Do not compare your answers until our next session.

1. *Wives only:* **What does submission to your husband in a Christ-centered marriage mean to you?**

   Husbands only: **What does being a godly husband mean to you?**

2. How would you describe you prayer life together as a couple?

3. How can your spouse be praying for you right now?

4. How often do you read the Bible?

5. What sin in your life right now is keeping you from being closer to God?

6. **What are ten things in your marriage for which you are thankful?**

7. **If you and your spouse have a major decision, what process would you use to insure you will make a God-honoring decision?**

CHAPTER 5

Developing an Intentional Marriage

The LORD will guide you always; he will satisfy your
needs—Isaiah 58:11

WE WERE MEETING WITH KEVIN and Michelle for a
Marriage Mentoring session. As we waited for Michelle to take
a restroom break, I (Ed) casually asked Kevin, a successful
financial advisor, what his secret was to finishing #1 in his
organization year after year. He said, "I get that question quite
often from other people in my industry. It is simple really. I
treat every client as if they were Bill Gates. Good customer
service is not enough. I create an *exceptional* client experience."
Ed then asked him a follow-up question. "What would your
marriage be like if you got up every day trying to make that day
exceptionally special for Michelle?" He responded
thoughtfully, "Great question." Michelle returned and our
session continued.

Several weeks later, after they completed the program,
Kevin and Michelle invited us over for dinner. After a delicious
meal as we were enjoying dessert, I asked Kevin what impacted
him the most from the marriage enrichment program. He
responded, "When you asked me what my marriage would be
like if worked on it as hard as I did my business. It was like a
switch flipped. I finally realized if I wanted my marriage to be
successful it required my attention."

God wants us to meet the desires and needs of our spouse.
Jesus gave us the perfect example of this when He humbled
himself to wash His disciples' feet. Jesus even washed Judas's

feet, and He knew Judas was about to betray Him. We need to follow Jesus' example and cheerfully, humbly serve our spouses with unconditional love. Agape love challenges us not only to serve, but also to do it sacrificially, placing our spouse's needs above our own. "Serve wholeheartedly, as if you were serving the Lord, not men" (Ephesians 6:7).

For us to demonstrate this servant's attitude in our marriage, we must change our motivation from "How can my spouse meet *my* desires?" to "How can I meet my *partner's* wants and needs?" We should love and respond with agape love by taking our focus off of ourselves. If Jesus, being God, took on the role of a humble servant (even unto death), why should we think we can live our lives for ourselves? We should each seek to glorify God with our life by having a servant's heart towards our spouse regardless of how they behave towards us.

When our loved ones fall short in meeting our needs, how we choose to respond will either bring us closer together or drive us apart. We cannot control our spouse's actions or responses. We can only control our own. The best way we can react is to choose responses honoring to God rather than responding to our partner in a hurt, angry, or passive-aggressive way.

Here are three ways to respond when our spouse doesn't meet our needs.

First, we must be certain that we have honestly and clearly communicated our desire to our spouse. We cannot assume that our spouse knows what we expect or need.

Second, we must determine if our expectation is reasonable. Unrealistic expectations are often fueled by our culture and cause disappointment and discontentment. When our expectations aren't reasonable, the best action is to lower them. People with reasonable expectations are happier than people who demand a lot of themselves and others, for demanding people are often disappointed. They tend either to hurt their relationships by nagging and dwelling on disappointments, or to suppress their emotions while feeling sorry for themselves. This self-absorption cultivates bitterness. We must accept instead of expect in order to have fewer disappointments and hurts. Sometimes the most loving thing we can do is to lower our desires and fill our minds with grace and unconditional, agape love towards our spouse.

If Jesus, being God, took on the role of a humble servant (even unto death), why should we think we can live our lives for ourselves?

Third and most significant, we need to turn our unmet expectations and needs over to God. If you feel your spouse is falling short of living out God's will in your marriage, take your disappointments to God. Ask God to work in your spouse's life. Ask God to help you to love your spouse with His unconditional love. Ask God to fill your needs when your spouse is unable or unwilling to. The Word of God tells us that Jesus Christ is sufficient to meet all of our needs. Philippians 4:19 promises, "And my God will meet all your needs according to his glorious riches in Christ Jesus." Instead of living with the disappointment and discouragement of unmet expectations and needs, we can look to God and His Word to fill our lives. God will never disappoint or fail us. When we learn to release our unfulfilled desires to God (and make them between God and us, instead of our spouse and us), God can fill us with His joy and contentment. Surrender to God your resentment, your disappointments, and your frustrations. Remember that only God is perfectly reliable. Just as you are imperfect, so is your spouse. God is still at work in both of you!

About eight years ago, Ed came up with an idea that demonstrates how to intentionally serve one another in love. He suggested that we start a weekly tradition of being king or queen for the day. This little exercise helps us understand and better communicate how we can each meet the other's needs and desires in our marriage.

We started by each choosing one-day a week that would be our special day. I (Angie) chose Friday. So every Friday I get treated like royalty. Ed wakes me up with a nice back rub; he warms my towel in the dryer and hands it to me as I exit the shower; he washes my car and fills it with gas; he sends me loving texts throughout the day. Saturday is Ed's day to be king. On Saturday I treat Ed like royalty. I wake Ed up with a back rub; bring coffee to him in bed; surprise him with sweet little love notes throughout the house; give him a head massage; run errands for him; and make him his favorite dinner. We both do many other extra special things for each other throughout the day.

At first, it was hard for me to tell Ed what I would like on my special day. I had a hard time feeling worthy. Over time, I realized that when we both give and receive a closer, more loving intimacy grows in our relationship. Today we have fun coming up with new and creative ways to treat each other

We must accept instead of expect in order to have fewer disappointments and hurts

special. The best outcome has been that this exercise ensures that if we get off track, we will be back on course by Friday and Saturday.

Just as Kevin shared at the beginning of this chapter, none of us would ever imagine a business being successful without intentional effort, yet most couples never put as much intentional effort into their marriages as they do other aspects of their lives. One of the greatest gifts you can give your marriage is to develop a life-long intentional attitude of serving one another in love.

Please answer the following questions independently of your spouse. Do not compare your answers until our next session.

1. Enumerate in order of importance your top five of the following ten needs identified by Dr. Willard F. Harley Jr. in his book, *His Needs, Her Needs*.

Order of Top Five Needs	Need
	Admiration
	Affection
	Sexual fulfillment
	Conversation
	Family commitment
	Financial security
	Honesty and openness
	Help around the house
	Recreational companionship
	Attractive spouse

2. **How can your spouse more intentionally meet the needs you outlined above?**

3. **When your spouse is not meeting your expectations and needs, how should you respond?**

4. **List at least five things you can do to be more intentional about improving your marriage.**

5. On a scale of 1 to 10, ten being the most, how good is your spouse about making you happy?

6. If one day your spouse said, "You are going to be king/queen for the day. Give me a list of five special things I can do for you today," what items would you list? What day of the week would you like to be your king/queen day?

CHAPTER 6

Finding the Sweet Spot in your Marriage

And there will be harmony between the two
—Zechariah 6:13

WE LIKE TO SAY THAT A MARRIAGE that is joyful is living in the "sweet spot." You are in the sweet spot when you and your spouse feel connected in all areas—emotional, physical, spiritual, and social. Everything is flowing in a positive way. Interaction is pleasant, happy, kind, and loving. There is harmony in the relationship. You are operating as a team, as one. The opposite from the sweet spot we call the sour patch. This is when the connectivity or oneness has been disrupted.

During a marriage mentoring session Brandon mentioned that it seemed his marriage to Mandy was great most of the time; however, when they would get into an argument it would sometimes take days or even weeks for them to get over it. Brandon and Mandy are a very bright couple, but when Ed asked what steps they would take to get back into their sweet spot, they had no answers. They just let it take its course and waited it out. Brandon and Mandy's situation is very common. They had love and commitment towards one another. They simply lacked the tools to get their marriage back on course when it got off track.

Marriages tend to have a momentum that moves them in either a positive or negative direction. When a marriage starts to spin in a negative direction, it takes an intentional effort to stop that momentum and get it moving back in a positive direction. There are specific skills and time-tested techniques that can be implemented by either a husband or wife to get their marriage back into the sweet spot. This chapter is about helping you understand some of these tools.

The following is a list of eighteen effective tools. Some are for keeping your marriage in the sweet spot while others are for helping you get back into the sweet spot. You may notice that some of these tools have been explained in previous chapters and some are new. This chapter has only three questions. In addition to answering these three questions, we want you to come prepared to explain each of the tools. This chapter is teaching a skillset that can make a life-changing difference in your marriage. Please do not cut corners—take time to learn these tools.

When a marriage starts to spin in a negative direction, it takes an intentional effort to stop that momentum and get it moving back in a positive direction

1. **Prayer.** When a couple has drifted into the sour patch and humbly comes before God together in prayer, they are more receptive to setting aside their individual agendas and selfish desires and to seeking the will of God who loves them and wants them to operate as one. Imagine how useful it would be to pray as a couple when things start to enter the sour patch. This should always be a tool for the man to consider as the spiritual leader of the family although a wife can always suggest praying together too.

2. **"I'm sorry. I win!"** Use this tactic to take advantage of your competitive nature and make a game out of forgiving quickly. Whoever says they are sorry first, wins! Now instead of letting little things fester, if one of you will quickly say sorry (knowing they just won), you can move forward with a smile. It's a great way to solve a problem and win at the same time. Angie and I (Ed) had cross words one day just as I was getting ready to leave for a meeting. Just after I left the house, I received a text from Angie that read, "I'm sorry." A few seconds later I received a second text that read, "I win!" It made me laugh and we were quickly back in our sweet spot.

3. **Fun.** For the health of your marriage, it is important to keep fun alive, but this is an area that will disappear when you are in the sour patch. Even if you are not feeling it, plan something fun that you both will enjoy doing together. The simpler the better. Some couples like going back to doing something they enjoyed when

they were dating. Couples should be able to bring out the playful child in each other. Laughter should flow freely. It has been said that fun is the litmus test for a good marriage. Good marriages have fun and marriages that have fun are good.

4. **Mad for five minutes.** There are times that you would like to let your spouse know that you are a little upset, but you don't want to make a mountain out of a molehill. An effective way to communicate your displeasure to your spouse and still keep things in perspective is to say, "I am going to be mad at you for five minutes." You both may laugh at the comment, but the point will be made.

5. **Act of kindness.** Doing a loving act of kindness towards your spouse when you are not feeling it is a great way to let your spouse know how committed you are to getting back into the sweet spot.

6. **Love graffiti on the mirror.** Use a dry erase marker to write a love note to your spouse. Keep an assortment of dry erase markers in your bathroom so you can be creative with your notes.

7. **"How full is your love tank?"** Ask your spouse, "On a scale of one to ten, how full is your love tank right now?" Follow up by asking, "What would it take to make it a ten?" (This one is especially good for us guys because it comes with instructions).

8. **Replace a criticism with an affirmation.** When you are tempted to criticize your spouse, stop yourself and instead replace the critique with a genuine affirmation. Criticism is one of the quickest ways to drive your marriage into the sour patch. By giving an affirmation, instead of making the situation worse, you make it better.

9. **Smile.** A simple smile can change the entire chemistry between a husband and wife. Smiling has so many positive effects, but smiles are often the first thing to disappear when a couple is not in the sweet spot. A smile will warm the heart of your spouse. A smile makes you appear more attractive. Studies have shown that smiling reduces blood pressure, lowers stress, boosts your immune system, releases endorphins,

It has been said that fun is the litmus test for a good marriage

makes you more positive, and builds confidence. Smiles are contagious, so be the initiator.

10. **Ten things I love about you.** In your first session you each made a list of "Ten Things I Love About You." When you are drifting into the sour patch, pull these lists out and re-read what you love about your spouse and what they love about you. Now that your heart is softened, ask your spouse to do the same. Now, each of you should add one more new thing to your list.

11. **Big picture.** When you and your spouse have an argument, ask yourself, "In the scope of eternity, does this really matter? For the sake of our marriage, can I just let it go?"

12. **Text.** Sometimes a loving text is all it takes to get back into the sweet spot. Recently Angie's phone was nearing the memory limit and she asked me to help her free some memory. I asked her if I could delete her text messages for the last two years. She said, "Yes, all except yours." She explained that occasionally she likes to go back and reread my loving text messages.

13. **King/queen for the day.** You learned this in an earlier chapter. Hopefully this is something you will incorporate into your weekly calendar. This is a relationship game-changer. It brings your relationship into the sweet spot at least two days per week.

14. **Special time.** Special time is one-to-one connected time together. It is also known as date night. It doesn't have to be fancy or expensive. It is just important to keep dating even after you get married.

15. **"I love you."** These words can be music to your spouse's ears. Add a hug and a long romantic kiss for extra credit.

16. **Start all over.** Occasionally you have a day that seems to go sideways from the start. When this happens, all it takes is for one of you to say, "Can we start over?" This is an agreement to start over with no talk of what may have caused the day to go wrong in the first place. This cannot be used for major problems, but is an excellent tool for small problems.

17. **Love and respect.** Women want to be cherished by their husbands and men want to be respected by their wives. As a husband, do something to make your wife

feel special. As a wife, do something for your husband to show him you are his biggest fan.

18. **Make it between you and God.** Make it between you and God instead of you and your spouse. Do the right thing because you want to be pleasing to God, even if you are not feeling it towards your spouse.

Michelle and Ron lost their sweet spot. They'd been married only eight months. They hadn't attended premarital counseling and now felt significant stress in their relationship. They came to us (Ed and Angie) and asked if we would mentor them. During our first session with them, it was clear that they were very much in love, but financial pressures from working multiple jobs to pay off their wedding debt were overwhelming them. They shared similar goals, but had no fun in their lives. In fact, they couldn't remember the last time they laughed or had a good time together since their wedding.

At the end of a serious first session, Ed gave them a homework assignment: go home and have a pillow fight sometime before the next session. When they arrived for session two, Ed asked them how their assignment went. They said at first, it was awkward. They knew we would hold them accountable, so they had to do it. Once they got started though, it wasn't long before they were laughing and giggling like kids. They eventually found themselves playfully wrestling on the floor. Michelle beamed as she said it was the first time in months they had enjoyed each other. Ron, with a little twinkle in his eye, remarked that it led to some of the best sex since their honeymoon! They were still under the same financial pressures as the week before, but they had a renewed sense of oneness and harmony that made the everyday pressures manageable as long as they were connected. They had found their sweet spot.

Dwelling in your sweet spot builds momentum in a positive direction. Conversely, dwelling in negative feelings and interactions builds momentum in a negative direction. It is up to you to take action to quickly return to the sweet spot in your relationship.

You may not use all of these tools; however, choose some that you can identify with and become proficient at them. Of course, there will be times in your marriage when these tools will not take care of the problem. In a future chapter on resolving conflict, we will share tools that will help address bigger issues.

Please answer the following questions independently of your spouse. Do not compare your answers until our next session.

1. **How would you define the sweet spot in your marriage, and when do you know you are in it?**

2. **You will be asked by your counselors to give a recap of the tools outlined in this chapter. Which tools mentioned are you most likely to use?**

3. **Share a memory of the two of you having fun together.**

Session III

Chapter 7 ❧ Personality Differences

Chapter 8 ❧ Differences between Men and Women

Chapter 9 ❧ Love Languages

CHAPTER 7

Personality Differences

I praise you because I am fearfully and wonderfully made—Psalm 139:14

DURING OUR PREMARITAL counseling, the pastor asked everyone in the group to raise their hand if they were compatible with their fiancé or fiancée. All twenty of us raised our hands high, only to have the pastor tell us we were all wrong. We were sure he was crazy. After all, we had known each other for eighteen months and were convinced we were perfect for each other in every way. The pastor explained that a great marriage is not based on a man and woman being perfectly compatible, but rather on a husband and wife learning to deal effectively with their incompatibilities.

Within just a few months of marriage, we knew what he meant. Instead of panicking and thinking we must have married the wrong person, we understood we must begin to gain skills to manage and cope with our incompatibilities.

Early in a relationship couples often say, "We have so much in common," "We love the same things," and "We agree on almost everything." Once married, they say, "We haven't much in common," "We don't understand each other," and "We can't seem to agree on anything."

Just as your spouse's similarities attracted you, so your partner's differences attracted you. You may have thought, "He will take care of our finances—he is more organized than I," or "She is more sensitive about others' needs than I am," or "He is more logical than I am about making decisions." Once married, these differences can become sources of friction. The differences that once seemed attractive now seem unattractive.

You think, "He is too controlling with the finances," "She is too sensitive about everything," or "He takes too long to make a decision." In other words, the differences that at first attract are what we later attack.

We are all created in the image of God. Yet we are also each unique and different. These differences are not right or wrong. In fact, the more we learn to embrace the differences we each bring into the marriage, the more we will understand how our different personalities complement and complete one another. God did not create any two people to be perfectly compatible. Our compatibilities (how we are the same as our spouse) as well as our incompatibilities (how we are different from our spouse) are both part of God's design for our marriage. They draw us into the oneness that God intended for us in marriage.

One way we grew to understand our personality differences better was by taking the Myers-Briggs Type Indicator® (MBTI®) personality assessment instrument. I (Ed) am systemized and organized. I like to plan detailed specifics before proceeding. To me, early is on time. I like to finish projects ahead of schedule. I feel strongly that before I can give myself permission to play, I need to finish all my work so that I don't have to come back to unfinished work.

Differences are not right or wrong

Angie, on the other hand, is happy to do her work and stop for play before the work is finished, even if it means she will have to work late into the night. Angie always had a hard time understanding why I put such pressure on myself. I had difficulty understanding how she could play before getting her work done.

When we took the MBTI®, we both had "aha" moments. We saw that we each had very different personality types in respect to how we manage our lives. We became more understanding and accepting of our different styles. We realized we both accomplish everything we needed to get done. We just approach it differently.

God created you and your spouse with unique personality differences, which reflect His image in each of you. These differences can bring marital understanding if we view the differences with respect and appreciation. Or these differences can cause marital discord if we view our way as the best or only way. When the differences become frustrating or even seem unbearable, talk honestly with your spouse. Speak gently, humbly, patiently, and lovingly. Allow these opportunities to draw you closer to your spouse and avoid letting resentment and bitterness develop. Above all, let God's grace and love prevail.

Please answer all of the following questions independently of your spouse. Do not compare answers until our next session.

1. **Do you believe you and your spouse are compatible? Explain.**

   (When finished with this question, proceed to the next page.)

2. **The statements below reflect personality traits. On a scale of 1 to 10, describe how well the statement applies to you.**

   1 = does not describe at all
   10 = very accurately describes me

	Statement	Rating (1–10)
A	I prefer to think things through carefully before moving in new directions.	
B	I enjoy being recognized publicly for my achievements.	
C	I generally don't like change.	
D	I have a daily to-do list and try to complete it.	
E	I am very spontaneous.	
F	I am very neat and tidy. I like things in their place.	
G	I am rarely late to an appointment, meeting, or event.	
H	I feel a sense of accomplishment when I complete a project. I am reluctant to start new projects until I finish the one I am working on.	
I	I prefer socializing in small groups (ideally with just one other couple), rather than at big parties.	

To further understand the personality differences between you and your spouse there are numerous online personality tests you can take. One such test is located at http://www.16personalities.com.

CHAPTER 8

Differences between Men and Women

*So God created man in his own image, in the image
of God he created him; male and female he created
them—Genesis 1:27*

"HE DOESN'T UNDERSTAND ME." "She is *always* so
emotional." "He won't share his feelings with me." "She
doesn't respect how hard I work to provide for the family."

Husbands and wives often feel misunderstood by their
spouse. You might be surprised to find out how the differences
between men and women are so extensive and wide-ranging.
Research findings can help us understand many differences,
but some we may never fully understand. God's creation has
many mysteries (including your spouse) that have yet to be
revealed!

This chapter looks at many ways men and women differ.
Despite the notable differences between the genders, God
created males and females equally and in His image. Some say
that men and women together portray many of God's
attributes. In simple yet profound ways, God designed your
differences to complement each other, which ultimately
enhances the oneness of your marriage relationship.

Just look at the titles of some of the books about the
differences between men and women:

- *Why Men Don't Have a Clue and Women Always Need More
  Shoes: The Ultimate Guide to the Opposite Sex*
- *You Just Don't Understand: Women and Men in Conversation*

- *Men Are Like Waffles—Women Are Like Spaghetti: Understanding and Delighting in Your Differences*
- *Men Are From Mars, Women Are From Venus: The Classic Guide to Understanding the Opposite Sex*

It's easy to see what a perplexing and challenging topic this is. Let's look closely at what research has found about these differences.

Gender Differences

Dr. John Gray, author of the best-seller, *Men Are From Mars, Women Are From Venus,* writes about the subtle differences between the brains of men and women:

> Men's brains tend to perform tasks predominantly with the left-side, which is the logical/rational side of the brain. Women, on the other hand, use both sides of their brains because a woman's brain has a larger corpus callosum, which means women can transfer data between the right and left hemispheres faster than men. … The other structural difference in men and women's brains is the limbic size, which controls bonding and nesting instincts. Females, on average, have larger, deep limbic systems than males. This is why Venusians [women] tend to be more in touch with their feelings and are better able to express them than men. The larger deep limbic system also increases a Venusian's [woman's] ability to connect and bond with others.
>
> The downside of this is that women are more susceptible to depression, not only because of the larger limbic system, but also because they produce less serotonin than men.[5]

Thus, scientific evidence shows differences in the brain structures of men and women and therefore differences in their reactions.

This is why women typically are better able to connect to others, are more in touch with their own feelings and the feelings of others, and are more nurturing than men. This means women are more likely to consider emotional ramifications when making decisions, while men typically consider logic.

---

[5] John Gray, "The Male vs. the Female Brain," posted April 27, 2011, ThirdAge.com, http://www.thirdage.com/love-romance/the-male-vs-the-female-brain (accessed June 23, 2012).

You may have noticed this in your marriage. For most decisions, husbands and wives benefit by looking at both emotional and logical perspectives. However, a wife should look at some decisions purely logically. Conversely, a husband should value the emotional perspective that his wife contributes.

When Trish and Bill described their marital relationship in my (Kathy Jo's) office, it was clear that their relationship had strengths. However, they had trouble understanding each other's parenting decisions. Trish wanted their daughter to attend a four-year university and to live away from home. She wanted her to have the "true college experience." Bill, not in agreement, wanted their daughter to attend the local junior college, get a job, and learn about the "real world."

Trish's opinion was based on her feelings and her own unmet dreams. She regretted having lived at home, worked part-time, and married before completing her college degree. Bill's solution was based on reasoning. He prioritized teaching his daughter responsibility through saving money while working part time. Together, they listened to each other's point of view, considered their daughter's maturity, and decided that both solutions were valid.

Ultimately, their daughter began attending the local junior college while working part-time. After saving money to offset living and tuition expenses, she transferred to a four-year university.

Since women and men process decisions and experiences differently (women relying more on emotions versus men relying more on logic), you'll need to put effort into communicating effectively. Using word pictures may help. For instance, Trish could have said to her husband, "When I lived at home instead of going away to college, I felt like a caged bird while my friends were spreading their wings by leaving home."

Jesus used word pictures when he spoke in parables. The book, *The Language of Love: How to Be Instantly Understood by Those You Love*, written by Gary Smalley and John Trent, explains how to use word pictures.

Here are some common generalizations about males and females that can help you understand each other. However, just as there are differences *between* men and women, there are differences *among* men and women, so some of these differences may not apply to your marriage.

Males tend to approach a problem in a more task-oriented, "let's-fix-it" approach. A man is more focused on solving the problem than on understanding the emotions associated with it. He will often make a decision based solely on the facts.

Females tend to approach a problem more creatively out of sensitivity to and concern for the feelings of those involved. A woman speaks from her heart, describing in great detail the emotional aspects of the problem. By processing the problem and venting her frustrations to her husband, she feels connected to him. Unlike men, women don't always want—or need—to find a solution.

છ

Males tend to view life in a linear or sequential way. He wants to focus on one event, situation, or problem at a time. Men compartmentalize the different parts of their lives.

Females tend to view life in a global way. She can focus on multiple events, situations, or problems in an encompassing way. A woman tends to integrate the different parts of her life and may handle all parts simultaneously. She is more likely to carry emotions from one area into another.

A man feels closer to others through sharing physical activities such as sports, hobbies, or tasks

છ

Males relate more shoulder-to-shoulder. A man feels closer to others through sharing physical activities such as sports, hobbies, or tasks. He enjoys doing activities with his spouse even if she is just there to observe. A man often feels closest to his wife after sexual intimacy.

Females relate more face-to-face. A woman is more interactive and relationship-oriented. She tends to focus on meaningful conversation, building rapport, sharing experiences, and asking questions. A woman often feels closest to her husband after emotional intimacy.

છ

Males receive their self-esteem and identity through career success and approval of work associates. He desires respect and support from his wife. A man wants his wife to be his number one fan and wants to operate with his wife as a team in marriage.

Females receive their self-esteem and identity from close relationships, especially from their husbands. Even if a wife feels good about many areas of her life, she wants to feel cherished by and special to her husband. A woman desires oneness in her relationship with her husband.

ᘒ

Males do not experience monthly hormonal changes. A man's role in the reproductive cycle—that of producing sperms—is not typically associated with emotional and physical symptoms.

Females may experience monthly hormonal changes associated with their menstrual cycle. Hormonal changes called premenstrual syndrome (PMS) typically begin five to eleven days before a woman starts her menstrual cycle. PMS refers to a wide range of physical and emotional symptoms, including mood swings, uterine cramps, food cravings, irritability, fatigue, and depression. A marriage benefits when a husband understands his wife's hormonal cycle.

Some of the differences between you and your spouse may surprise you. Just the mere fact that a man's brain is wired differently than a woman's brain means that men and women think, speak, relate, and make decisions differently. Not understanding sexual and hormonal differences causes conflicts and disappointments. Recognizing your differences and embracing how together you have the ability to be the best team is rewarding.

ᘒ

Even if a wife feels good about many areas of her life, she wants to feel cherished by and special to her husband

Please answer the following questions independently of your spouse. Do not compare your answers until our next session.

1. How do the general differences between men and women affect your decision-making process in marriage?

2. Men and women get their self-esteem in different ways. Taking this into consideration, how could you help strengthen your spouse's self-esteem?

3. Women have conversational needs in marriage that differ from men's. Has this created a problem in your marriage? If so, how? What solutions do you suggest?

4. Do you believe that PMS (Premenstrual Syndrome), menopause, or any other hormonal factors are a factor in your marriage? If so, explain.

CHAPTER 9

Love Languages

*Above all, love each other deeply, because love covers
over a multitude of sins—1 Peter 4:8*

INSIDE YOU IS AN EMOTIONAL love tank. If it is full, the
whole world looks bright and you dwell in your sweet spot.
When your love tank is not filled by those most important to
you, the world looks gray. If your love tank is half empty, you
feel neglected and unloved. This is when people may go
looking for love in all the wrong places.

There are many ways to express and receive love. What
speaks love to your spouse may be different from what speaks
love to you. Gary Chapman's book, *The Five Love Languages*,
explores this topic. He says that the best way to love someone
is to love them the way they want to be loved. In other words,
speak to them in their love language.

We intuitively speak to our partner in the language we like
to receive, which is not necessarily our partner's love language.
This is like a boy buying his mother a football for Christmas.
If you've ever received a different reaction from your partner
than you expected when you said or did something thoughtful,
this may be why. In your mind, you were expressing love, but
since you were not speaking in your spouse's love language, you
did not make any emotional points. You can give yourself credit
for trying, but this chapter's objective is to get you speaking
fluently in your spouse's love language so that his or her love
tank stays full.

The first time we (Ed and Angie) taught this concept was
with Heather and Ryan during their premarital counseling.
They lived an hour and a half apart. Their schedules brought

them together only once per week when we met them for counseling. Heather was a task-oriented, high achiever. She had gone through college and obtained her MBA in just four years. As they came together each week, she gave Ryan a quick hug and kiss, and then immediately asked Ryan if he had completed the task list she had given him for their wedding preparations. His joy in seeing her would immediately deflate.

It was no surprise to learn that Heather's primary love language was acts of service. Ryan scored very low on acts of service. His primary love language was physical touch. Heather scored zero on touch (zeros are very rare). As they discussed their love languages test results, they shared how they had each experienced a draining of their love tank by the other: Heather, when Ryan didn't complete his list; and Ryan, when the list seemed more important to Heather than the two of them coming together affectionately.

Six months later, they invited us over to see their new place and look at their wedding photos. As we enjoyed coffee and dessert, they cuddled on the family room floor and could barely keep their hands off each other. It was very cute and quite a change. We asked them what their favorite part of their premarital counseling had been. Heather immediately responded, "The love languages session. Learning to speak in Ryan's love language was like giving me the key to his heart." During that session, her eyes had opened to how important physical touch was to him. Heather had not grown up in a family that displayed affection through touch. She was truly enjoying this newfound expression of affection. Ryan also realized that acts of service were important to her. She adjusted the lists she gave him to just a few things each day, and he dutifully made sure everything was accomplished. They had each learned how to keep the other's love tank full in ways that were at first not natural to them, and they grew closer than ever in the process.

When you understand the concept of speaking in the right love language, you'll find you can apply it to your family and friends and enhance those relationships, too (for other family members, you can access the Love Languages Test for free online at http://www.5lovelanguages.com). You will find great joy in filling other people's love tanks. After all, "It is more blessed to give than to receive" (Acts 20:35).

Below is a definition of each of the five love languages.

Learning to speak in Ryan's love language was like giving me the key to his heart

1. **Words of Affirmation.** This involves providing honest, authentic, genuine, and focused compliments and positive, affirming words of encouragement. These help build another's self-image and confidence.

2. **Special Time.** Show someone how much he or she means to you by setting aside special time with your full and undivided attention to just be together, focus on each other, and participate in shared activities and experiences.

3. **Gifts.** This often gets a bad rap. People who love through or with gifts appreciate any type of gift, large or small. The emphasis is on the thought behind the gift, not the extravagance of the gift.

4. **Acts of Service.** Communicate that you truly care for, enjoy, and appreciate your spouse by going out of your way to joyfully serve him or her by completing activities without being asked.

5. **Physical Touch.** Whether it is a simple touch on the shoulder, a gentle hug, or a passionate kiss, physical touch is a powerful method for communicating your love and comfort with someone.

Please take the Love Languages Test that applies to you: "The Five Love Languages Test for Wives" is in Appendix 4 and "The Five Love Languages Test for Husbands" is in Appendix 5. Enter your results in the table below. Do not share your results with your spouse until your next session. Finish by answering the three questions at the end of this chapter.

℘

Results to Love Languages Test

Count how many times you circled each letter and enter the result in the Letter Tally column. Add all results and confirm they total 30. Find the highest tally and put a "1" in the Primary column to its right: that's your primary love language. Find the next highest tally and put a "2" in the same column. That's your secondary love language.

Letter	Letter Tally	Primary	Love Language
A			Words of Affirmation
B			Quality Time
C			Receiving Gifts
D			Acts of Service
E			Physical Touch
Total:	30		

Please answer the following questions independently of your spouse. Do not compare your answers until our next session.

1. On a scale of 1 to 10, how full is your love tank?

2. What could your spouse do to raise it to a 10?

3.   Complete this sentence, "I feel most loved when ..."

Use the three questions above to occasionally test how well you are meeting each other's needs and to know how you can better meet those needs.

Session IV

Chapter 10 ❧ Family and Extended Family

Chapter 11 ❧ Communication

Chapter 12 ❧ Resolving Conflict

CHAPTER 10

Family and Extended Family

You shall rejoice in all the good things the LORD
your God has given to you and your household
—Deuteronomy 26:11

THE RELATIONSHIP DYNAMICS between spouses is challenging enough. When we add children, siblings, parents, in-laws, grandchildren, and grandparents, life can become very complicated. In this chapter, we will look at the dynamics of your nuclear family (you, your spouse, and any children) and of your extended family. As you reflect on these, you may be surprised at how significantly these relationships impact your marriage.

Our nuclear family has life stages. Our home may be bustling with the sounds of children. We may be married without children. Perhaps we are empty nesters. Maybe we are married with children from previous marriages. Or it could be that we are struggling with the challenges of infertility. No matter what life-stage you find yourself in, the one over-riding principal in marriage is: Make your spouse a priority and your most important relationship.

Children

Parenting comes with challenges. As much as children are blessings, they also exhaust our energy, time, and financial resources. Many spouses (especially husbands) feel neglected by their partners when children enter the picture. It is important that the husband-wife relationship remain the most important relationship in the family unit, despite the attention and care children need.

This is not an easy task. Be intentional about creating private time together. There is tremendous truth in the saying, "One of the greatest gifts you can give to your children is to love your spouse." Schedule date nights and other blocks of uninterrupted time without children regularly.

Constantly evaluate and discuss parenting topics. Rarely do couples agree perfectly on all of each day's decisions and family rules. Guide your decisions by the values and goals that you want to impart to your children. Strive to always appear united as parents, and discuss any differing parenting views behind closed doors.

Parents

Make your spouse a priority and your most important relationship

Let's talk for a moment about our extended family members, especially our in-laws and parents. Your marital relationship takes priority over families of origin. Family obligations may cause stress between you and your spouse. If they do, establish some healthy boundaries. This may feel uncomfortable, but will meet the overall goal of prioritizing your spouse.

Jim and Debbie came into my (Kathy Jo's) office exhausted and discouraged. They both had demanding careers, and after three years of marriage, they had a hard time articulating what was wrong. So many parts of their relationship were going well: they had found a new small group with other young couples, they both loved their challenging jobs, and they looked forward to trying to have children soon.

Jim described his family of origin as tight-knit. Most of his family—including his parents and three siblings—lived within a few miles of each other. The extended family gathered for birthdays, anniversaries, holidays, and Sunday night dinners just about every weekend.

Although Debbie enjoyed Jim's family, she felt overwhelmed, tired, and lonely. She longed to have some alone time for herself (before marriage, she enjoyed reading a new book nearly every week) and she also missed the special dates she and Jim took during their dating years. It didn't take long for them to realize that between their demanding jobs and extended family activities, there was little or no time left to relax or to cultivate their marriage relationship.

Jim and Debbie realized that they needed to establish some protective boundaries. They began to say no to some of the Sunday night dinners. At first declining was uncomfortable, but the family understood. They decided to take a romantic vacation to a nearby beach resort instead of going on the annual family trip together that Jim's parents were planning—a fabulous cruise to Alaska. This was the first trip just the two of them had taken since their honeymoon. They let their family know they would rejoin the family vacation the next year. Within months, their adjustments left them feeling more balanced in life and more connected in marriage.

Here are some helpful guidelines for maintaining healthy, positive interactions with extended family members:

- **Support your spouse by delivering difficult or disappointing news to your own family of origin** if you need to set boundaries (especially turning down family events).

- **Establish a positive tone when you come together.** Greet your family members in a way that makes them feel special. Years ago, a very sweet lady, Amelia, mentored me (Angie). Every time I went to her house, she and her husband stopped whatever they were doing and exclaimed with glee, "Angelita's here!" Their warm, excited greeting always made me feel special. I decided this was something I wanted to extend to my own family. I immediately began cheerfully greeting Ed and our sons with an exuberant hug whenever they entered the house. Our adult sons now have homes of their own, but they can still count on a delighted Mom and Dad ready to greet them joyfully!

- **Face family challenges together.** Support your spouse in ways that will demonstrate your interest and care. Avoid minimizing, dismissing, or ignoring your spouse's concerns. Often, listening to your spouse's anger, discouragement, disappointment, sadness, or fear is the best action you can take. Be a safe person with whom your spouse can honestly share.

- **Remember that you cannot control the way your extended family interacts with you and your spouse.** However, you can control the way you respond to them. Seek reconciliation when disagreements occur. You and your spouse may hope family members will change undesirable behaviors, but the best predictor of future behavior is past behavior so change is unlikely. If it becomes necessary to protect one of you, pray for God's love, grace, and forgiveness as you set appropriate boundaries.

- **Speak positively about your spouse and don't share marital problems with family members.** It is easy to seek support from family members when you are frustrated, but after the conflict is resolved and you and your spouse have moved on, your family may have difficulty forgetting the hurt your spouse caused you. If you need to share marital frustrations with someone, choose a trusted, same-sex friend or seek church or professional support.

Speak positively about your spouse and don't share marital problems with family members

Julie and Steve had been married for twenty-one years when they arrived in my (Kathy Jo's) office. They had been separated for several months, following the devastating news of Steve's infidelity. Julie asked Steve to move out of their home while she processed her hurt and anger. She told Steve she needed time to make decisions about the future. Steve moved back home with his parents. He began to talk to his parents, especially his mother, about his problems with Julie, seeking support and justification for his affair.

During the separation, Julie confided in her parents and her sister. She admitted that she needed to talk to someone in the family just about every day because she just didn't know what to do with the myriad of feelings she was having. Julie also began to share with her seventeen-year old daughter, Lisa, all the problems and suspicions she had felt about her husband. Julie knew instinctively that it wasn't right to pull her daughter into her marital mess—after all, Steve was also Lisa's father—but it was just too tempting and too convenient to resist getting Lisa's support and comfort, especially in the evening when Julie couldn't stop crying.

When Julie and Steve began counseling, the family had mixed emotions. Julie's family didn't think Julie should give Steve another chance. They warned her that he would probably have another affair: "Once a cheater, always a cheater," they said. Lisa, their daughter, found it extremely difficult to forgive her father. She was angry that her father would cheat, lie, and hurt her mother in such a terrible way. In fact, Lisa said she would never trust another man (including her father) ever again!

After a long process of healing and rebuilding trust, Steve and Julie decided to stay in their marriage and work on developing a "new" marriage. The family members were not, of course, a part of the difficult, insightful counseling sessions that took place. Steve and Julie began to understand why the affair happened, but they rightfully resisted telling their family members their counseling session details. Their family involvement complicated and made more difficult their recovery. Each family member had personal feelings about the affair. It would have been far better if Steve and Julie had not talked about their marital problems to family members, especially their daughter.

Your relationship with your children and extended family could potentially bring you endless joy or tremendous stress and disappointment. Make your marriage a priority. Unite on all family decisions. Pray for God's help and wisdom as you face challenges together.

Please answer the following questions independently of your spouse. Do not compare your answers until our next session.

1. **If you have children, do you put the children or your spouse first? Explain.**

2. **If you have children, what are the biggest areas of parenting in which you and your spouse disagree?**

3. Describe the relationship you have with your parents. How has this relationship shaped or impacted your marriage?

4. Do you ever share marital problems with a family member?

5. What issues with your extended family are creating problems in your marriage? How can you and your spouse work together to change the situation?

- Bring a picture of your extended family to this week's meeting.

CHAPTER 11

Communication

*Do not let any unwholesome talk come out of your
mouths, but only what is helpful for building others
up according to their needs, that it may benefit those
who listen—Ephesians 4:29*

COMMUNICATION IS TO THE relationship what blood is to
the human body. It is vital and it is life sustaining. But just as
human bodies can die if an infection spreads to vital organs
through the bloodstream, so marriages can die if destruction
spreads to vital parts of a relationship through communication.
Practicing effective, healthy communication is crucial to a
thriving marriage.

Couples often share strong feelings about how their
communication skills have deteriorated, saying things like,
"You never listen to me. When I start to talk, you just interrupt
me." "We just end up arguing about everything. What's the
use?" "You don't even try to talk to me anymore. You just start
yelling!"

When couples struggle within their relationship, they often
say they have poor communication skills. The fact is couples
are continually communicating whether they realize it or not.
A door slammed in anger, a sigh, a roll of the eyes, even the
silent treatment are all ways that we communicate. We send
messages by what we *do* say and what we *don't* say. Unhealthy
communication is not the problem as much as a symptom of
the problem. In this chapter, we will discuss six components of
healthy communication.

Communication consists of five components: content, tone, body language, timing, and listening. In other words, communication involves *what* we say, *how* we say it, the *body language* we use while saying it, *when* we say it, and *how* it is heard. Let's look at each component and how it contributes to successful, loving communication.

Content refers to the words we use to communicate our thoughts. Our words are the primary instrument that we use to communicate quickly, effectively, and precisely. Many problems can arise with content. We may struggle with expressing our thoughts or feelings in the right words. Men and women differ in how they communicate content. You may think that you have communicated one thing, while your spouse has understood your words in a completely different way.

Tone refers to the volume and inflection we use when communicating. Tone can change the meaning of the content. It is the punctuation of our spoken word. (Imagine how difficult it would be to write without punctuation.) Tone communicates many things, including enthusiasm, disinterest, and anger.

Sometimes we find ourselves speaking at a volume that seems inoffensive to us, but which our spouse perceives differently. As Jeff and Susan talked in my (Kathy Jo's) office, at one point Susan turned to Jeff and stated, "Don't talk to me with that tone of voice." Jeff responded with surprise, "What do you mean? I didn't even raise my voice." Later the tables turned when Jeff said to Susan, "You don't have to be so angry." To this Susan responded with exasperation, "I am not angry. I am just frustrated that you aren't listening to me." Each of them had not realized how much their tone was affecting the conversation.

We need to always be aware of how our tone of voice reflects criticism, blame, or sarcasm—all of these can be destructive to our marriage. If your spouse raises his or her voice, a good technique for de-escalating the volume is to lower your own voice: "A gentle answer turns away wrath, but a harsh word stirs up anger" (Proverbs 15:1). We should be more aware of the tone we use in conversation with our spouse and use it to reflect productive emotions like concern, care, support, and unconditional love.

We need to always be aware of how our tone of voice reflects criticism, blame, or sarcasm—all of these can be destructive to our marriage

Body language refers to the position and movement of our bodies when we communicate. It is the form of language that is non-verbal.

> One study at UCLA indicated that up to 93 percent of communication effectiveness is determined by nonverbal cues. Another study indicated that the impact of a performance was determined 7 percent by the words used, 38 percent by voice quality, and 55 percent by the nonverbal communication.[6]

Non-verbal communication is the form of communication that is most involuntary; therefore, it is usually the most honest. Non-verbal messages are communicated through gestures, postures, facial expressions, and other behaviors. You might not be a body language expert, but quite often you can intuitively sense what others are saying through their non-verbal messages. Here are some body language tips you can use to communicate more positively:

- Make eye contact with your spouse when you are communicating.
- Use physical touch to express approval, care, concern, or support. A loving touch can help your spouse feel safe in sharing their emotions.
- Study your spouse's non-verbal communication. It may speak volumes to you—without even a word spoken.
- Be aware of what your non-verbal gestures are communicating, both negatively and positively. Are you expressing a loving, caring, and respectful attitude, or a critical, defensive, unapproachable stance?

Timing refers to when you choose to communicate. You can be clear in content, tone, and body language, but if you select a poor time, you can be ineffective, or worse, you can communicate the opposite of what you intended.

During our (Ed and Angie) mentoring session on communication with Brad and Sandy, Brad said that Sandy had a bad habit of dropping bombshells on him just as they arrived at church. She would save difficult news such as, "Oh, by the way, my parents are coming over this afternoon for dinner," to tell him then because she knew he wouldn't have time to

---

[6] Susan M. Heathfield, "Listen With Your Eyes: Tips for Understanding Nonverbal Communication," About.com, http://humanresources.about.com/od/interpersonalcommunicatio1/a/nonverbal_com.htm (accessed June 25, 2012).

respond. But this made matters worse because he not only received bad news but felt sabotaged in the process.

There is real truth to the saying, "Timing is everything." It is good to choose your timing wisely when communicating about sensitive issues. Choose times when you are not tired, rushed, or preoccupied. Be careful not to talk about sensitive issues when children are present.

Listening is one of the most important components of effective, healthy communication. Everyone desires and needs to be heard. When spouses don't listen to one another, the result is often frustration, anger, misunderstanding, and hurt. Poor listening skills can be an inherited family trait. If you or your spouse were raised in an environment where family members did not listen or were unable to express their feelings, you will likely have some challenges communicating and listening effectively. If this is true of your family of origin, don't be discouraged. You can change the patterns of your past and build new patterns with effort and practice.

Communication expert, Michael P. Nichols, says, "Genuine listening means suspending memory, desire, and judgment—and, for a moment at least, existing for the other person."[7] Be alert to some of the common blocks to listening: judging, daydreaming, advising, reading someone's mind, filtering (selective listening), planning your response, and changing the subject (through blaming, being defensive, or being passive aggressive). Good listeners listen with an open mind. They are careful not to judge their spouse's feelings as right or wrong. They are careful not to judge their spouses' motives, following Paul's teaching to the Corinthians, "Therefore judge nothing before the appointed time; wait till the Lord comes. He will bring to light what is hidden in darkness and will expose the motives of men's hearts" (1 Corinthians 4:5). They listen with their full attention instead of planning their response. One way to communicate that you are listening is to paraphrase back to your spouse what you have heard. This is called *reflective listening*. The Bible says it best: "Everyone should be quick to listen, slow to speak and slow to become angry" (James 1:19).

At times we need to communicate a hard truth to our spouse. Accountability is crucially important in our battle

---

[7] Michael P. Nichols, *The Lost Art of Listening: How Learning to Listen Can Improve Relationships* (New York: Guilford, 1995), 64.

against sin. Proverbs 27:17 says, "As iron sharpens iron, so one man sharpens another." Who better to hold us lovingly accountable than our spouse? This type of critique should never be given in haste or in anger. It should only be done in a lovingly honest way. When considering whether or not you need to confront your spouse ask yourself, is it true, is it necessary, and is my approach going to be loving and kind? Although biblically reproving your spouse may seem intimidating and difficult, if you bring it before God, He will give you the grace you need to accomplish it. Remember, you too are a sinner, so above all, approach your spouse humbly. Not always, but most of the time, when we correct our spouse in the right way, it turns out better than we anticipate and draws us closer together in the process.

If you, like Jeff and Susan, are frustrated in your attempts to communicate effectively, don't give up. Take the five components of communication—content, tone, body language, timing, and listening—and practice the areas that need improvement. Then as Ephesians 4:15 encourages, "Instead, speaking the truth in love, we will in all things grow up into him who is the Head, that is, Christ."

Is it true, is it necessary, and is my approach going to be loving and kind?

Please answer all of the following questions independently of your spouse. Do not compare answers until our next session.

1. **On a scale of 1 to 10, ten being best, how would you rate your spouse's listening skills?**

2. **Does your spouse often interrupt you?**

3. **Would you say you criticize your spouse seldom, sometimes, or often?**

4. How often does your spouse criticize you?

5. Give an example of when your spouse was brutally honest instead of lovingly honest with you. How could he or she have communicated better in that situation?

6. Which of the communication styles below describe your spouse? Circle all that apply.

   a. Communicates with lack of detail.

   b. Communicates with excessive detail.

   c. Communicates with a loud or angry voice.

   d. Fails to communicate things that I should know; for example, does not tell me about a work trip he/she must take until days after he/she knew of it.

   e. Often does not communicate what he/she is really thinking.

   f. Communicates things that are intentionally hurtful.

   g. Retreats and stops communicating at all.

   h. Other_____.

7. **When you are in the sweet spot in your marriage do you still experience communication problems?**

CHAPTER 12

Resolving Conflict

When a man's ways are pleasing to the LORD, he
makes even his enemies live at peace with him
—Proverbs 16:7

WHEN WE ARE WORKING with a premarital couple and
they declare, "We get along perfectly with each other," or "We
rarely disagree," I'm more concerned than relieved. One of the
greatest myths of marriages is that happy, successful couples do
not fight. The truth is that a strong marriage relationship isn't
afraid of conflict. Instead, the spouses feel safe expressing what
bothers them, and they work together to resolve differences. In
other words, conflict doesn't destroy marriages: the inability to
resolve conflict does.

Although we strive for peace in our marriage, we are
destined to have some conflict. Numerous factors contribute to
conflict: our sin nature, sharing physical space, and having
ideas, desires, and preferences that collide. Though
disagreements are inevitable, conflict should not build walls of
resentment or erupt into full-out wars, but instead should be
opportunities for growth and understanding.

Our different personality types and behaviors learned from
our family of origin play into how we are conditioned to
respond to conflict. Three common unhealthy responses are:

Win—Your goal is to win the conflict. This is the "I win; you
lose," or "I'm right; you're wrong" position. Your
spouse's opinion and feelings take second place to your
need to win. This displays your competitive side—your
goal of always winning or your "I know it all" side—

instead of considering or listening to your spouse's point of view.

Withdraw—Your goal is to withdraw from conflict. This is the "I don't care" position. You may see no hope in resolution or you don't want the conflict to escalate. Above all, you want to avoid the discomfort of dealing with the conflict, so you withdraw physically or you give your spouse the silent treatment in a passive-aggressive way.

Yield—Your goal is to yield to conflict. This is when you go along with your spouse's demands or agree with their position rather than risk a confrontation. Once again, you want to avoid the discomfort of conflict. You would rather stuff your feelings and give in than argue with your spouse. You minimize or dismiss your own needs and opinions, not wanting to take a stand against an angry or demanding spouse.

There are problems with all of these unhealthy responses. Instead of encouraging peace in your relationship, these unhealthy responses promote frustration, resentment, and anger. God wants your marriage to cultivate oneness through committing to work together as a team in every area of life. If one person's personality or preferences are squelched while the other always gets his or her way, you're not working as a team. To keep a relationship strong, both people need to feel heard. Your marriage relationship must be based on absolute honesty and openness. The goal is not to win, withdraw, or yield, but to resolve conflict—often through compromise—with respect and love.

You have likely noticed not all conflicts require major confrontation. This does not mean that you avoid conflict; it only means that small conflicts often resolve themselves easily. As the saying goes, "Don't make a mountain out of a molehill."

During marital counseling, Debbie and Cody shared a recurring situation. Whenever Debbie needed a break or had plans that did not include their two young children, Cody agreed to stay home with the kids. But when Debbie returned home, she always argued with Cody about how he had cared for the kids. Whether they ate the wrong foods, watched too much television, didn't take a nap, or made a mess of the house—Debbie always had a barrage of complaints. This disheartened Cody and made him feel always criticized, even when he was trying hard to be helpful.

Not all conflicts can be resolved easily—especially when anger, blaming, or defensiveness is present. Bigger conflicts or recurring conflicts that go unresolved will eventually bring bitterness and resentment. Conflicts will fester if ignored.

By using some conflict resolution skills that we are going to teach in our next session, Cody and Debbie were able to arrive at a peaceful solution. Instead of expecting Cody to do everything her way, Debbie could let go of her own expectations and be grateful for Cody's willingness to care for their children.

If you are experiencing continual unresolved conflict in your marriage, remember that God's Word challenges us to restore peace. "'In your anger do not sin': Do not let the sun go down while you are still angry" (Ephesians 4:26). When we obey this command, we resolve our conflicts in a timely manner. God wants to be involved in every aspect of our life, including conflict resolution. Invite God in to take control, be sensitive to His leading, and pursue peace.

Here are some suggestions to consider when resolving conflict with your spouse:

Conflict does not destroy marriages. It is the inability to resolve conflict that destroys marriages.

- Don't always insist on being right or having the final say. If you are right, no defense is needed. If you are wrong, no defense will do. Consider a "win-win" position—where you and your spouse compromise and come to a solution that benefits both.

- Focus on the present. If you're holding on to old hurts and resentments, your ability to see the reality of the current situation will be impaired. Focus on what you can do in the here-and-now to solve the problem.

- Instead of thinking that your spouse needs to change or that you are incompatible, concentrate on the changes that you can make. Remember that conflicts are opportunities for growth—in you and your spouse.

- Know when to let something go. If you can't come to an agreement, agree to disagree. Above all, pick your battles. Consider whether the issue is really worth your time and energy.

- When a conflict arises, look for a lesson that God may be teaching you. If you give your spouse his or her way in a decision, even if the decision turns out to be bad, God will still work in your lives.

- Make a promise that no matter how angry you become with your spouse, you will never threaten the marriage by speaking of, or alluding, to divorce.
- Be ready to forgive and forget and to move past the conflict without holding resentment or anger. Refer back to chapter 3 for more information on forgiveness.

Remember, conflict does not destroy marriages. It is the inability to resolve conflict that destroys marriages. Conflict can trigger strong emotions that lead to hurt feelings, disappointment, and discomfort. When handled in a healthy way, conflict has the ability to increase our understanding of one another, to build trust, and to ultimately strengthen our marriage.

When you meet with your mentor couple for this session, they will give you a specific formula involving ten steps that will help you and your spouse resolve conflicts.

Please answer the following questions independently of your spouse. Do not compare answers until our next session.

1. **What is the difference between a discussion and an argument?**

2. Name one or more minor conflicts in your relationship that do not need to be resolved (a minor conflict is a conflict that does not cause harm to the marriage, or a conflict that will go away on its own).

3. List one or more moderate conflicts in your marriage (a moderate conflict is a conflict that does not threaten a healthy marriage, but its resolution would generate more harmony).

4. List one or more major conflicts in your marriage (a major conflict is a significant issue that if left unresolved would damage a healthy marriage; or a recurring conflict that continually causes dissension).

As part of your homework assignment please go to www.marriagebygod.org and watch the *Conflict Video*. You may watch the video together if you wish.

Session V

Chapter 13 ❧ Emotional Intimacy

Chapter 14 ❧ Physical Intimacy

Chapter 15 ❧ Affair Proofing Your Marriage

CHAPTER 13

Emotional Intimacy

Two are better than one—Ecclesiastes 4:9

MICHELLE CAME INTO MY (Kathy Jo's) office frustrated and discouraged about her marriage. She didn't see any solution to her unhappiness, emptiness, and loneliness. She was conflicted about ending her marriage, but divorce seemed like her best option. With tearful eyes, she said, "Kevin and I have been married for over ten years—we live and sleep together every day—but I don't feel like I really *know* him. And he certainly doesn't know me at all." She continued, "It isn't that he has done anything really wrong. It's just that we are so distant, more like roommates than two people who are supposed to be close." It didn't take long to conclude that the biggest problem in Michelle and Kevin's marriage was their lack of emotional intimacy.

Intimacy often refers to the physical, or sexual, relationship in a marriage. However, *emotional intimacy* and *sexual intimacy* are not synonymous. Emotional intimacy is about being comfortable and safe enough to share your innermost thoughts and feelings. It is about expressing your fears, hopes, and dreams without facing judgment. Perhaps the best way to define emotional intimacy is to remember the phrase "into-me-see."

Michelle craved knowing Kevin, and Kevin knowing her, on more than a superficial level. She wanted them to readily share their struggles and concerns, as well as their joys and successes. She wanted to lovingly discuss their big decisions and decide them together. The emotional intimacy she yearned for involves both partners sharing vulnerably as well as listening with understanding and empathy.

In this chapter, we will examine the necessary elements for experiencing emotional intimacy. We will also look at some of the common roadblocks that hinder closeness in marriage. You'll evaluate the level of emotional intimacy in your own marriage.

God created us in His image, including being made with some of the same relational characteristics as the Triune God. We have the capacity and desire for connection, closeness, community, and dependency. God planned for married couples to meet many of each other's needs for love and connection through the oneness of marriage. Emotional intimacy cultivates oneness. Satin's number one attack on marriages is to destroy the oneness in marriage.

Some of the most important elements of emotional intimacy are unconditional (agape) love, commitment, trust, respect, honesty, and vulnerability. Emotional intimacy exists when two people are committed to the well-being and development of each other, fully trust each other, and know they are perfectly safe with each other.

Fear is one of the biggest deterrents to emotional intimacy

Fear is one of the biggest deterrents to emotional intimacy. Fear can come in many forms: the fear of rejection, judgment, losing control, appearing weak, or getting a negative response. God does not want us to fear emotional intimacy in our marriage for any reason. This type of fear is not from God. "There is no fear in love. But perfect love drives out fear, because fear has to do with punishment. The one who fears is not made perfect in love" (1 John 4:18).

Sometimes hurts and traumas from our past cause fear or make it hard for us to trust others. If this is true, you can improve your marriage by working on healing those wounds. Relationship experts and marriage counselors Milan and Kay Yerkovich have devoted much of their life's work helping couples understand how early life experiences can impede their ability to love correctly and thus affect their intimacy:

> Many people who lacked deep emotional connection as children resist looking back, some of them even go to the point of denying that the past is significant. Yet, in many cases, the stronger the resistance to looking back, the greater that need actually is … the entire point of our work: to put the past in the past so we can get on with our present lives. But the simple fact

is that before we can learn how to love correctly, we need to see clearly how the past has shaped us.[8]

This imprint from our family of origin shapes our behaviors, beliefs, and expectations of all relationships, especially our marriages. Consider how your early experiences of care and comfort (or lack of care and comfort)—especially from your parents—have shaped your ability and your desire for connection and closeness.

Numerous behaviors and responses can be roadblocks to emotional intimacy. Here are some of the most common:

1. **Being independent** is when a husband or wife tends to be private, is unwilling to share thoughts and feelings, appears self-sufficient, prefers taking care of his or her own needs, and does not involve a spouse in decision-making. A couple should strive for neither independence nor overdependence, but rather healthy interdependence.

2. **Being avoidant** is when a husband or wife withdraws when upset; prefers to not deal with conflict; and perhaps becomes angry if his or her spouse expresses emotions or needs. The other spouse often feels emotionally detached from the avoidant spouse. Placating is a form of being avoidant: attempting to avoid conflict or hostility by making concessions or appeasing.

3. **Being passive aggressive** is when a husband or wife prefers to be passive (silent) rather than express honest feelings or directly confront issues, but then acts out in negative ways. People who are passive aggressive don't always exhibit outward anger or appear malicious— instead they may procrastinate, blame, sulk, be chronically late, and resist accomplishing requested or expected tasks.

4. **Being sarcastic** is when a husband or wife jokes around by saying the opposite of what they mean. Sarcasm is criticism and is often accompanied by negative attitudes such as disapproval, contempt, scorn, and ridicule. Sarcasm in marriage can be annoying, hurtful, and destructive.

---

[8] Milan and Kay Yerkovich, *How We Love: Discover Your Love Style, Enhance Your Marriage* (Colorado: Waterbrook, 2011), 24.

The behaviors detailed above are detrimental to growing intimacy in marriage. Other damaging behaviors to oneness include self-pity, non-biblical criticism, defensiveness (inability to listen to another's point of view), and excessive anger. All of these behaviors are sinful.

If the emotional intimacy you desire with your spouse needs improvement, start by taking a look at your own actions and behaviors. Sin is one of the biggest obstacles that blocks emotional intimacy in marriage. Get quiet before God and ask Him to reveal any sin in your life that may be disrupting your closeness. Vulnerability with your spouse begins with vulnerability with God. We can only truly embrace the "two hearts becoming one" relationship by placing God at the center of our relationship and being fully submitted to Him. If you are struggling with sin, confess it to God and repent. Then humbly share your struggle with your spouse in a transparent, honest conversation. The discussion questions at the end of this chapter will help get you started.

Vulnerability with your spouse begins with vulnerability with God

By the way, Michelle and Kevin (our couple from the beginning of this chapter) worked together in a dedicated way throughout their sessions and made great progress. Michelle came to understand that she pushed Kevin away with unrealistic expectations, nagging, and demands for attention. Instead of telling Michelle how he felt about her demands, Kevin withdrew by watching television and purposely avoiding Michelle. Kevin learned this behavior from his passive father, who was rarely available in his own life.

After acknowledging their inappropriate behaviors, Kevin and Michelle slowly began to share their true feelings and were able to learn how to be comfortable with asking for what they needed. Michelle learned new ways to express her feelings without nagging. Kevin learned how to express his needs, which included having some alone time. No longer did Michelle feel lonely and empty. By improving their ability to be vulnerable, to understand each other, and to know each other, they slowly began to enjoy spending more time together.

Emotional intimacy does not mean you will see everything eye-to-eye with your spouse. Instead, it means that when you disagree (which should happen in a healthy marriage), you can still be sensitive to your partner's point of view. Emotional intimacy gives confidence to discuss differences within a safe environment and to compromise together when necessary. This way of sharing develops a deeper knowledge and understanding between you and your spouse ("into-me-see"). Don't forget, the more emotionally intimate you are with your spouse, the more likely you both will reach out to meet each other's needs. May this be the kind of intimacy that you experience in your relationship!

Please answer the following questions independently of your spouse. Do not compare answers until our next session.

1. **Rate the accuracy of the following statements with:**

   A = Almost-always
   S = Sometimes
   N = Needs improvement

Statement	Rating
I feel emotionally connected and understood by my spouse.	
I feel comfortable and safe sharing my deepest thoughts and feelings with my spouse.	
I trust my spouse to keep my confidences.	
I feel my spouse knows me better than any other person.	
We make important decisions together as a team.	
We hold each other accountable in a God-honoring way.	
We pray together as a couple on a regular basis.	

2. What behaviors and responses hinder emotional intimacy in your marriage (such as avoidance, sarcasm, passive-aggressive behavior, criticism, nagging, anger, or family-of-origin imprints)?

3. What would improved emotional intimacy in your marriage look like? What changes would you like to take place?

4. Complete this statement, "This is what I would like you to know about me in order to understand me better ..."

CHAPTER 14

Physical Intimacy

I am my lover's and my lover is mine
—Song of Songs 6:3

WHEN GOD FIRST PLACED Adam and Eve in the Garden, they were fully connected in both physical and emotional oneness. Genesis 2:25 says, "The man and his wife were both naked, and they felt no shame." In his book, *A Celebration of Sex*, Dr. Douglas Rosenau comments insightfully on this passage:

> It is tremendously moving to think of God's original one-flesh companionship. Adam and Eve, before the fall of Eden, had the marvelous capacity of being totally naked, physically and emotionally, with no shame or fear. They reveled in a childlike trust and curiosity—laughing, exploring, giving and receiving love. Sex was a glorious, innocent celebration lived out with instinctual honesty, respect, and zest for life. It was naked and unashamed with no performance anxiety, inhibitions, pain, or selfish skill deficits. What a relationship and sex life they were able to have as they truly "knew" each other, inside and out![9]

Different from any other relationship, God gives a husband and wife the sexual union as an exclusive way to express their love for one another. The Song of Solomon is a beautiful, descriptive book found in the Old Testament, which focuses on the sensuous coming together of a husband and wife in eros love. Through the Song of Solomon, we understand what God thinks about sex—and it is good!

---

[9] Douglas E. Rosenau, *A Celebration of Sex* (Tennessee: Thomas Nelson, 2002), 4.

Sadly, Satan often takes God's goodness and distorts it. God wants us as a Christ-centered couple to diligently protect our marriage bed; otherwise mistrust, misunderstandings, insecurities, inhibitions, and feelings of betrayal can invade your marriage. Clear and honest communication with your spouse about your sexual needs is the best way to overcome any threats to your relationship.

Communication and sex are uniquely intertwined in marriage. Not only is communication the key to having a fulfilling sexual intimacy in marriage, God uses the physical intimacy between a husband and wife to communicate love, commitment, caring, understanding, fun, forgiveness, and intimate friendship. It is one of the most intense and important ways a husband and wife express their exclusive oneness. Neglecting this area of your marriage deprives you and your spouse of the special union that God desires for you. Below are some things to consider and perhaps discuss:

The biology is different between men and women. When it comes to sex, family therapist Gary Smalley describes men as microwave ovens and women as Crock-Pots®. Most men can achieve an orgasm in just a few minutes of focused concentration and stimulation. However, it usually requires an average of ten to thirty minutes of focused concentration and appropriate stimulation in order for a woman to reach a sexual climax. Due to these differences, you will want to understand your spouse's needs. Additionally, it is not important that both partners always reach an orgasm to have a fulfilling sexual experience. Because of the additional time and focus needed for a woman to climax, sometimes a woman can have a fulfilling experience by just sharing physical and emotional closeness.

Be honest with your spouse about your sexual needs and wants. Mutually satisfying sexual intimacy requires being both selfish and unselfish. Great lovers know their own bodies and enjoy their sexual feelings, as well as knowing and meeting those of their partner. Ask your spouse what would make sexual intimacy more pleasurable for him or her and share what is pleasing to you. Remember your spouse cannot read your mind! Sharing your needs and wants will not take the romance out of your sexual experience. On the contrary, it allows for better sexual intimacy. Your spouse will gain more enjoyment if he or she knows that you are experiencing sexual fulfillment

God uses the physical intimacy between a husband and wife to communicate love, commitment, caring, understanding, fun, forgiveness, and intimate friendship

too. The goal should be to combine the best of what you both desire to celebrate a rich sex life together.

Men and women have different emotional and sexual desires and needs. Although a husband and wife are meant to meet each other's emotional and physical intimacy needs, God created them with different needs and responses. In general, a woman needs to feel a sense of emotional intimacy with her husband in order to desire him sexually. If a wife is experiencing tension with her husband, or is physically exhausted, making love will likely be the last thing on her mind. Conversely, a man will be drawn into a stronger emotional intimacy with his wife through sex. A man will likely still be sexually attracted to his wife and desire sexual intimacy even when there is tension in the marriage. If he is feeling exhausted, he probably won't want to invest in emotional intimacy, but he may enjoy engaging in lovemaking as a release from tension and exhaustion.

Husbands should invest in creating an emotional oneness with their wives as the first step in foreplay. Consider setting the environment early in the day through a loving note, calling from work to say "I love you," listening to her and connecting with her emotionally, relieving her of some of the demands of her daily chores, or providing time for her to unwind with a bubble bath. A husband will honor God by being a student of his wife, developing a greater capacity for emotional intimacy, and giving special attention to the environment that will light her fire.

Use your five senses—sight, touch, sound, smell, and taste. God has designed our sexual relationship with our spouse to be enjoyed through our senses. Be creative and invest time in finding ways that you can use your senses to create an exciting sex life! Here are a few ideas:

- **Sight.** Create soft lighting. Because men tend to be visually stimulated, wives should consider choosing lingerie that their husbands will enjoy. Women should also be comfortable with their husbands viewing them naked.
- **Touch.** Make sure the room is at a good temperature. A gentle massage can be a good way to get things started. Pay attention to neglected areas like ears, neck, inner thighs, etc. Use massage oil, or softly tickle with a feather. Use your imagination …
- **Sound.** Music can be a sensuous way to set the mood. Keep the CD player loaded with your favorite romantic tunes.

- **Smell.** Odors can make or break a sexual encounter. Be sure to practice good hygiene. Put on your spouse's favorite perfume or cologne. Create a wonderful aroma through candles.
- **Taste.** Like smell, taste can be memorable. Be sure you have fresh breath. Sip your favorite beverage. Have some of your favorite taste treats to lead into a romantic evening.

The five senses can create an amorous environment, but they can also kill the mood: the television blaring under bright lights, with a possibility of being interrupted by children or time constraints will not be the environment conducive for most (especially women) to fully enjoy a romantic encounter. Use your imagination with all your five senses and keep your sexually intimate times full of fun and variety!

Self-acceptance, self-esteem, and a good body image are important. There has never been anyone else God created who is just like you! He designed us to have individual gifts, talents, and abilities, and we need to embrace our physical differences. As Christians, we should honor God by having a good self-image—accepting ourselves without comparing ourselves to others. Women tend to do this most. No matter how beautiful others may tell a woman she is, she still tends to feel insecure about her looks. Remember, your spouse was attracted to you above anyone else.

Pay attention to your health, maintain good hygiene, and incorporate regular exercise into your life to help your body image. Equally important is to accept the natural changes that occur through life changes, such as pregnancy, health conditions, or aging.

Keep your spouse's sexual needs a priority. The sex drive between husbands and wives is rarely equal. There will be times when one spouse (usually the husband) will be more interested in sex than the other. Agape love involves selflessness. Look to meet your spouse's sexual needs even if you are not in the mood because it is the loving thing to do.

Wives should understand that the physical need for their husband to engage in regular sex is different from their own. *Focus on the Family* advises wives this way:

> One of the biggest differences between you and your husband is the fact that he experiences sex as a legitimate physical need. Just as your body tells you when you're hungry, thirsty, or tired, your husband's body tells him when he needs a sexual release. ...

Immediately after sexual release, men are physically satisfied. But as their sexual clock ticks on, sexual thoughts become more prevalent, and they are more easily aroused. The physical need for sexual release intensifies as sperm builds in the testicles. … The best way for a woman to understand this dynamic is to relate it to another physiological need. If you've had a baby, you may relate to the experience of milk building up in your breasts a few days after giving birth. The buildup of breast milk becomes annoying (and even painful) until the milk is expressed. … Just as with breast milk, sperm production tends to "keep up with demand." The more often a man has sex, the more semen his body is likely to produce.[10]

After a number of days without sex, a man commonly feels neglected by his wife and concludes she doesn't care for him as much as for her other priorities. He will likely become irritable. He may even become resentful. A wise wife will not ignore her husband's sexual needs. She will offer her body as a gift, not using excuses such as being too tired, being too busy, or having a headache. (In fact, studies have shown that sexual activity can be the best medicine to get rid of a headache.) She may, at times, meet her husband's needs through quick encounters (quickies) to satisfy his need for release. Other times, though, they should slow things down for a more mutually pleasing encounter. And sometimes the couple may want to make a special occasion of the event.

Another significant detail that plays into a couple's sexual fulfillment is the rise and fall of testosterone during a woman's monthly menstrual cycle. This varies significantly throughout the month and will affect her sexual desire and enjoyment. Below are some fun facts shared by Gabrielle Lichterman, author and founder of *Hormonology*. They identify the specific days of a women's menstrual cycle when sex will be most enjoyable. A husband and wife might benefit from paying attention to this monthly cycle.

[10] Juli Slattery, "Sex Is a Physical Need," Focus on the Family, http://www.focusonthefamily.com/marriage/sex_and_intimacy/understanding-your-husbands-sexual-needs/sex-is-a-physical-need.aspx (accessed June 25, 2012).

The Hormonology Guide to Sex

- **Red Hot Days**: Day 1 (first day of menstruation) to Day 14 (ovulation), peaking on Day 13 and remaining high on Day 14.
- **Lukewarm Days**: Day 15 to Day 23
- **Bonus Red Hot Days**: Day 24 to the end of her cycle.
- **Ultimate Time For Sex**: The morning of Day 13. "The morning is when a man's testosterone peaks in his 24-hour hormone cycle. And Day 13 is when testosterone peaks in a woman's monthly hormone cycle. When these two hormonal peaks intersect, they can set the stage for the best sex all month long," states Lichterman. [11] Mark your calendars!

There are natural age-related changes to our bodies that can impact our sexual enjoyment as a couple, such as menopause and erectile dysfunction.

Menopause can cause physical symptoms such as vaginal dryness, hot flashes, disruptive sleep, lower energy, and emotional feelings of anxiety, sadness, loss or depression. Each woman is unique in how menopause affects her. According to the Mayo Clinic, menopause can happen in your 40s or 50s, but the average age is 51 in the United States.[12] The symptom of vaginal dryness can usually be managed through the use of water-soluble lubricants. Dietary adjustments, cardiovascular exercises, lifestyle changes and hormone replacement therapy are also beneficial in minimizing the symptoms of menopause. Women should seek counsel from their gynecologist on the best form of treatment for their symptoms.

According to the Massachusetts Male Aging Study, about 40% of men experience some degree of inability to have or maintain an erection at age 40 compared with 70% of men at age 70.[13] There are a variety of treatments available to men who

---

[11] Armen Hareyan, "Women Can Now Predict When They Will Have The Best Sex," January 20, 2006, EmaxHealth, http://www.emaxhealth.com/48/4247.html (accessed June 25, 2012).

[12] Mayo Clinic Staff, "Menopause," Mayo Clinic, http://www.mayoclinic.org/diseases-conditions/menopause/basics/definition/con-20019726.

[13] William C. Shiel Jr., reviewer, "A Picture Guide to Erectile Dysfunction, July 13, 2013, MedicineNet.com, http://www.medicinenet.com/impotence_pictures_slideshow_erectile_dysfunction/article.htm, slide 4.

have erectile dysfunction. A man should consult with his doctor to determine the best treatment. Lifestyle changes such as exercise, weight loss, avoiding alcohol, and giving up smoking are recommended too.

Physical intimacy should be a celebration of your one-flesh companionship. Husbands and wives should come together with a childlike trust and curiosity—laughing, exploring, and giving and receiving love. If that is not how you would describe the last time you were sexually intimate together, discussing the following questions should help you begin to enjoy one another in new and exciting ways.

Please answer the following questions independently of your spouse. Do not compare answers until our next session.

1. **Are you currently enjoying sexual intimacy with your spouse in the joyful way described above? If not, what is the underlying factor? (Some examples might be life stressors, fatigue, lack of desire, negative response from spouse, poor body image, performance anxiety, pain, health issues, medication, or lack of emotional intimacy.) Explain.**

2. **Do you feel comfortable discussing your sexual needs with your spouse?**

3. Do you feel comfortable being naked in front of your spouse?

4. Do you desire sex more or less frequently than you and your spouse currently engage? Do you think your spouse desires more or less sexual intimacy?

5. What are some creative ways you can keep the romance alive in your relationship?

CHAPTER 15

Affair Proofing Your Marriage

*Marriage should be honored by all, and the marriage
bed kept pure, for God will judge the adulterer and
all the sexually immoral—Hebrews 13:4*

"I COULD NEVER HAVE AN affair! Affairs only happen to *other* couples." If that is how you feel, then the first thing you need to recognize is that *no one* is immune to an affair. The truth is that most couples that have experienced an extramarital affair are caught off guard. They never planned to have an affair.

In the general population, some reports suggest an astounding 50 to 60 percent of husbands and an equally shocking 45 to 55 percent of wives have had an affair by the time they are forty.[14] The incidence of infidelity between Christians is probably close to that of the general population.[15] An additional study of pastors sponsored by *Christianity Today* found that 23 percent of the 300 pastors surveyed admitted to some form of sexually inappropriate behavior with someone other than their wives while in the ministry.[16] Because infidelity is so pervasive, our own marital faithfulness demands our ongoing attention.

God is clear that the marital bed should be kept pure (Hebrews 13:4). Sexual sin includes not only physical adultery,

---

[14] Grant L. Martin, "Relationship, Romance, and Sexual Addiction in Extramarital Affairs," *Journal of Psychology and Christianity* 8, no. 4 (Winter 1989): 5.

[15] Dave Carder, *Torn Asunder: Recovering from an Extramarital Affair* (Chicago: Moody, 2008), 25.

[16] D. J. P. Huson, "Predictors of Infidelity among Pastors" (master's thesis, Biola University, 1998).

but also lusting. Jesus said, "You have heard that it was said, 'Do not commit adultery.' But I tell you that anyone who looks at a woman lustfully has already committed adultery with her in his heart" (Matthew 5:27–28). The *Merriam-Webster Dictionary* defines lust as "an intense longing or craving." A quick, passing thought about someone being attractive is not a sin, but an excessive craving or lusting after someone is akin to committing adultery in the eyes of God.

God's warnings about adultery and His command to be faithful in marriage is why your marriage needs protection. Just as you cannot inoculate against the flu after you come down with it, you cannot inoculate against an affair once it has happened. Protecting your marriage involves establishing boundaries that should be defined, implemented, and respected at all times.

Jennifer was excited to be on a team from her church that was preparing for a mission trip. Her husband was unable to take the time off from work to go along. The team prepared for months before their departure. They met weekly because there were so many decisions to make about the trip and it was important to get to know the other team members. Joey, who was recently divorced, was one of Jennifer's favorite new friends on the team. He seemed to share Jennifer's passion and commitment to make a difference through the mission's ministry. Jennifer found herself looking forward to the team meetings and seeing Joey.

One night Jennifer and Joey started to talk about their personal lives. Joey shared about his disappointment with his failed marriage. Jennifer told Joey that though she loved her husband, he didn't seem interested in hearing about the mission trip and he was always preoccupied with his job. Soon they were both drawing emotional support from each other. They felt like they understood each other so well. Unfortunately, the mission trip provided an opportunity for their closeness to develop more. Neither Jennifer nor Joey planned to be sexually intimate, but it just moved in that direction one night on the trip. This is how easily an innocent situation can escalate into an affair.

Jennifer neglected to protect her marriage. Joey, though divorced, encouraged an inappropriate relationship. Both were lonely and vulnerable. Without boundaries, it was easy for the relationship to become susceptible to the affair. We strongly

Just as you cannot inoculate against the flu after you come down with it, you cannot inoculate against an affair once it has happened

recommend the following ten protections for your marriage to guard against becoming vulnerable to an affair:

1. **Keep Christ at the center of your marriage.** This includes attending church together, reading the Bible together, and most importantly, praying together.

2. **Fulfill your spouse's emotional and physical needs.** Understand your spouse's needs and seek to meet them. Additionally, understand your own needs and communicate them.

3. **Spend as much time together as possible.** Intentionally set a tone at home that makes it a place that you and your spouse enjoy. Find fun activities to share together. Plan regular date nights. Your marriage should be based on a solid friendship where you enjoy being together.

4. **Do not spend too much time with one couple.** Statistics show that affairs often happen between couples that spend a lot of time together, with a high incidence between best friends.

5. **Do not share your marital problems with anyone of the opposite sex.** A husband should not discuss his marital problems with another woman, and a wife should not discuss her marital problems with another man. Decide in advance to never engage in this type of conversation. Do not let anyone of the opposite sex discuss marital problems with you, either.

6. **Stay away from singles environments.** Problems can occur when you do activities with single friends that involve them seeking to meet new people of the opposite sex. The different lifestyles between singles and married couples are typically not compatible. Always be with others who encourage your marriage commitment.

7. **Save all of your physical affection for your spouse.** Kissing on the lips and intimate hugs should be reserved for your spouse. If you don't know the difference between a friendly hug and an intimate hug, ask your spouse.

8. **Guard your heart and your mind.** Internet connections can start out innocent, but they pose the same threat to relationships as in-person encounters. Be sure to honor the same boundaries online as you do in

person. Set boundaries with your Facebook account, and always provide your spouse complete access to your computer. Be alert to any people or opportunities that may tempt your mind to have lustful thoughts. The Internet gives immediate access to pornography. Try to go to bed together to avoid late night Internet temptations. If you are tempted to view these resources, seek out the accountability of a mature Christian friend. Get the help of a professional, if needed.

9. **Avoid significant friendships with someone from the opposite sex.** Couples often enter marriage with a close friend of the opposite sex. Once married, meeting or communicating with this friend alone is no longer appropriate. The workplace can also present situations where you work closely with a co-worker of the opposite sex. Be sure to keep the conversation appropriate, avoid social interaction outside of work, and guard your heart. If your spouse is uncomfortable with a relationship you have with anyone of the opposite sex, respect your spouse's feelings and discontinue it.

10. **Realize that your marriage is not immune to an affair.** Never let your guard down. Affairs happen to people who least expect it. Set boundaries to protect your marriage and observe them with conviction.

Keeping the home fires warm is one of the best ways to protect your marriage. A marriage is most vulnerable to a spouse seeking validation outside of the marriage when things get cold at home. Remember, you play a big part in how your spouse esteems him- or herself and consequently how he or she thinks about the marriage. Be sure to admire and cherish one another and continue to operate as a united team. When love is felt at home, there is no need to go looking for it elsewhere.

Please answer the following questions independently of your spouse. Do not compare your answers until our next session.

1. **In which of the following ways do you engage with friends or work associates of the opposite gender**

one-to-one without the knowledge of your spouse? Check all that apply.

- ☐ Phone calls
- ☐ Email
- ☐ Texting
- ☐ Commenting on Facebook posts (or other social media)
- ☐ Private messaging through Facebook (or other social media)
- ☐ Coffee breaks
- ☐ Meals/drinks together
- ☐ Business meetings
- ☐ Social events

2. List 5 activities or hobbies you would enjoy doing with your spouse.

3. Is there any relationship outside of your marriage that you can identify as needing additional boundaries? What action steps would you suggest putting into place to improve your hedges?

4. What is your attitude towards pornography?

5. Do you and your spouse have total access to each other's technology activities? Do you occasionally check each other's Internet history?

6. Are you comfortable with the amount of time that your spouse spends away from you? Explain.

Session VI

Chapter 16 ❧ Finances

Chapter 17 ❧ Marriage Goals

Chapter 18 ❧ Keeping the Flame Going

CHAPTER 16

Finances

*No servant can serve two masters. Either he will hate
the one and love the other, or he will be devoted to
the one and despise the other. You cannot serve God
and Money—Luke 16:13*

JOHN WALKED AT THE BEACH with his wife, Carrie, thinking the relaxed setting would make discussing finances easier. When they saw a man with dirty hair and ragged clothes drinking from something hidden in a brown paper bag, John said to Carrie, "You see that guy there? He is worth $15,000 more than we." Shocked, Carrie said, "What's he doing homeless?" John explained, "He's a drunk worth nothing, but we're $15,000 in debt."

Many couples today are in debt. It's one of the most prevalent problems in marriages. Numerous studies show that money is the number one reason why couples argue. Studies also show that money is the leading cause of divorce. Our schools teach many subjects, but seldom offer classes in money management. Yet, not knowing calculus or French won't threaten your marriage as will poor money management.

The Bible says much about financial management. In fact, money is the second most common theme found in the Bible—only the Kingdom of God is mentioned more. As we begin this session on financial principles, let's dispel three common money myths.

Myth 1: Money is the root of all evil. In the Bible, it is not money that is evil, but loving money: "For the love of money is a root of all kinds of evil" (1 Timothy 6:10).

Focusing on money leads to greed, selfish ambition, and pride. Jesus said, "No servant can serve two masters. Either he will hate the one and love the other, or he will be devoted to the one and despise the other. You cannot serve both God and Money" (Luke 16:13).

Myth 2: It is a sin to be rich. The Bible does not say it is a sin to be rich. Many prominent and righteous people in the Bible were among the richest people of their day: Abraham, Joseph, Job, King David, and King Solomon. In reality, "The earth is the LORD'S and everything in it" (Psalm 24:1). We are merely stewards of God's possessions.

Myth 3: It is a sin to be poor. Some believe that if they have enough faith, God will bless them with financial riches along with anything else they desire. Some call this the name-it-and-claim-it theology. They believe that a lack of wealth is the result of a lack of faith. Or they may believe those who lack wealth lack God's favor. The truth is that God does not promise wealth and riches to those who are faithful. God does, however, promise to meet our *needs*: "And my God will meet all your needs according to his glorious riches in Christ Jesus" (Philippians 4:19).

Studies show that the average American family will spend over 80 percent of their income repaying debt

The United States leads the world in many areas, especially finances, yet the average American saves less than individuals in any other industrial country. According to *Business Week Magazine*,[17] Americans save, on average, 3.9 percent of their disposable income, compared to 11.7 percent saved by the Germans, 14.3 percent by the Swiss, and 38 percent by the Chinese. Most Americans would be unable to survive financially if they had to go without income for six months.

This lack of savings carries adverse consequences. For example, when emergencies arise (and they will), a missing savings cushion stresses and strains both the budget and marriage. Couples may be forced to borrow money, incurring debt payments and interest fees. Studies show that the average American family will spend over 80 percent of their income repaying debt.

---

[17] Christopher Power, "How Household Savings Stack Up in Asia, the West, and Latin America," posted June 10, 2010, BloombergBusinessweek Magazine, http://www.businessweek.com/magazine/content/10_25/b4183010451928.htm (accessed June 25, 2012).

Most couples have financial problems for one of these reasons:

Lack of financial planning or organization. The proverb, "Failing to plan is planning to fail," is often attributed to author Alan Lakein. We tend to be emotional about money. When emotions are high, it's easy to make fiscal mistakes. However, if we develop a plan when we are not emotionally charged, we are more likely to work together towards our goals.

Lack of financial knowledge. We should be lifelong students of financial principles. It is important that both husband and wife stay informed about the family finances.

Lack of financial independence. When we become adults, we normally become financially responsible for ourselves. This transition is not always easy, and sometimes there are setbacks. If you and your spouse find yourselves dependent on others—perhaps due to unforeseen circumstances—strive for financial independence. Don't rely on a future inheritance, which is another form of financial dependence, for circumstances can change and the inheritance might not come or might be less than expected. We should always practice good stewardship by living within our means at our current income.

Lack of facing our financial reality. We might be telling ourselves that we will start to manage our money wisely after we make "just one last purchase." This is like thinking that we will start a diet tomorrow after one more splurge on a one-pound box of chocolate today! Sometimes people procrastinate beginning good money management because they would rather be in denial about their financial situation. Unfortunately, one more purchase digs the debt hole that much deeper.

Lack of financial contentment. No matter how much we have, it's easy to want just a little more. The Apostle Paul wrote, "I know what it is to be in need, and I know what it is to have plenty. I have learned the secret of being content in any and every situation, whether well fed or hungry, whether living in plenty or in want"

(Philippians 4:12). We should practice focusing on being appreciative to God for what we have.

Lack of ability to delay gratification. More than ever, we live in an instant gratification generation—fast food; video on demand; instantaneous pain relief; and buy now, pay later. We want what we want and we want it NOW! The ability to make immediate credit card purchases enables easy debt. We need to discipline ourselves with our finances.

Many believe financial security is based on how much income we make in our careers. That's only one factor among several: how much you make, how much you spend, and how wisely you save and invest. You cannot always control how much you earn. You can, however, limit how much you spend, determine how much you will save, and plan for how much you will invest.

Consider how two couples' decisions affected their financial security and future:

Trevor and Julie were both public school teachers. They had three children. Trevor worked summer school every year and brought in extra income by teaching driver's training before and after school. Except for their house and cars, they bought nothing they couldn't afford to pay for at the time of purchase and thus avoided paying high interest rates. They paid their credit cards in full every month. They bought used cars and drove them at least seven years. By careful planning they were able to take a nice vacation every year with their kids (in later years even traveling to Australia). When interest rates went down, they refinanced their home into a fifteen-year loan. By the time they retired at age sixty-five, they owned their home free and clear, both cars were paid off, and all three kids had graduated from state colleges. They looked forward to a comfortable retirement.

Cliff and Andrea both made substantial incomes in sales jobs, often receiving large bonus checks. They had one daughter, Sarah. Because of their demanding jobs they frequently ate out; had a gardener and a housekeeper; took their cars to the car wash weekly; and had most of their clothes dry-cleaned. They believed that since they were in sales, appearance was important. They wanted to show how successful they were, so every three years they leased new Mercedes. Every year they enjoyed both an exotic tropical vacation and a cruise. As their home appreciated in value, they refinanced and took money out to support their lifestyle. When the economy plunged, so did their incomes. They continued to spend at the same level by using credit, expecting the economy to improve soon. Modifying the spending habits developed in prosperous times proved difficult. By the time Sarah was ready for college, they were heavily in debt with no equity in their home. Although they had always promised to pay for Sarah's attendance at a four-year private university, their only option was for her to live at home while attending community college. Later, Sarah took out student loans to finish two years at a local state college. With little savings, Cliff and Andrea withdrew retirement funds to pay off emergency bills, incurring tax penalties. They reached 65 knowing they'd need to postpone retirement many years.

Cliff and Andrea made substantially more money over the years than Trevor and Julie. Yet Trevor and Julie managed their money responsibly. They made conservative, careful choices in how they spent, saved, and invested their money, living in ways that encouraged a secure financial future.

A Few Tips to Help You with Your Planning

- Borrowing is not a sin, but bondage to debt is. It makes you a slave to the lender. "Let no debt remain outstanding, except the continuing debt to love one another" (Romans 13:8).
- The average American family receives over thirty offers for credit cards each year; the average credit-card debt per household is $15,956.[18] Many of us need plastic surgery: we need to cut up the cards that enable us to acquire debt.

---

[18] Ben Woolsey and Matt Schulz, "Credit card statistics, industry facts, debt statistics," posted February 28, 2012, CreditCards.com, http://www.creditcards.com/credit-card-news/credit-card-industry-facts-personal-debt-statistics-1276.php (accessed June 25, 2012).

- Your checkbook's ledger reveals your financial values. See if your ledger reflects the values you wish to display.
- Before you make a purchase, ask yourself three questions: (1) Do I really need it? (2) Can I afford it? (3) Is it worth it?
- Any time you spend money, visualize the purchase in one-dollar bills. Credit cards, debit cards, and checks make spending money too easy.
- Calculate your net hourly wage. When you consider a purchase, calculate how long you would have to work to buy it. If you make twenty dollars per hour gross, you probably make thirteen dollars per hour net. If dinner and a movie cost forty dollars, you would have to work over three hours to pay for them.
- Live each day as if it were your last, but plan your finances as if you'll live forever.
- Make sure you have insurance to protect against catastrophic loss: health, life, disability, auto, and homeowner's or renter's insurance. To save money, get higher deductibles. Make sure your upper limits cover your total assets.
- Begin with term life insurance to get the most coverage for your dollar.
- Have only one credit card (unless you need one for business—then have two).
- Avoid purchasing anything with a credit card unless you have the money to pay for it when the bill comes due. Interest on credit cards is exorbitant and cannot be deducted in your taxes.
- Sometimes money is used as an unhealthy way to control a spouse. Never use money as a means to get power or control.
- Keep the ledger in your checkbook current. Before you write a check, enter the check amount into the ledger and balance it. This way, you always know your current balance.
- *The Millionaire Next Door* says most millionaires live in their homes for twenty years. Most have never spent more than $400 on a suit or $250 on a watch. Millionaires are not extravagant spenders, but neither do they deprive themselves. They are just not into trendy consumerism, which is the worst kind of consumption because it costs the most money. It could be said that a rich person is not the

Your checkbook's ledger reveals your financial values

one who has the most material goods, but the person who is content with the least.

You May Need Financial Counseling If …

If you fall into one of the following four categories, you may need professional help:

- **Impulsive spender.** If you often buy things that catch your eye that you don't need, you may be an impulsive spender.
- **Compulsive spender.** If you have an irresistible urge to spend money when you are upset, you are a compulsive spender. Your attention is more on the act of shopping and spending than on purchasing needs.
- **Special-interest spender.** If the stereo in your car is more expensive than your car, you may be a special-interest spender. It's okay to spend discretionary income on a special interest you enjoy (most people do), but do it responsibly and within budget.
- **Status-seeking spender.** If you spend money you don't have on items you don't need to impress people you don't like, then you may be a status-seeking spender.

What are the Three Best Investments?

#1   **Invest in God and His work.** All money and wealth is God's. Billy Graham said, "God has given us two hands—one to receive with and the other to give with. We are not cisterns made for hoarding; we are channels made for giving."[19] You cannot out give God.

#2   **Invest in a home.** A primary residence is the only investment you can live in, receive tax deductions from, and sell after living in it for only two years, having the entire profit tax exempt (up to $500,000 per couple). In addition, you can take advantage of the principle of leverage. To understand leverage, look at these two scenarios:

"God has given us two hands—one to receive with and the other to give with"
—Billy Graham

---

[19] Billy Graham, "Billy Graham Quotes," BrainyQuote, http://www.brainyquote.com/quotes/authors/b/billy_graham.html (accessed June 25, 2012).

o You purchase a home for $500,000 cash. The home appreciates 10 percent. The return on your investment of $500,000 is $50,000, or 10 percent.

o You purchase a home for $500,000. You put $100,000 down and finance the balance. The home appreciates 10% on the full value of the home. The return on your cash investment of $100,000 would be $50,000 or a 50 percent return. So you receive a 50 percent return instead of a 10 percent return. This is the principle of leverage.

#3   **Invest in a retirement account.** Research shows that 87 percent of Americans will be unable to retire at sixty-five. Many couples do not make their retirement account a priority. They postpone investing, believing they can address it later when they have extra money. However, it is best to begin building a retirement account as early as possible—some believe even before buying a home. A retirement account allows pre-taxed income to be deposited into an investment without paying taxes on the initial investment or the gain until the funds are removed in retirement. The amount you defer on taxes each year gains interest. You can take money out during retirement in ways that let you pay taxes at a lower rate.

After investing in God, a home, and a retirement account, you can discuss other investment options. Here are some tips:

- **Stay away from get-rich-quick schemes.** They seldom work and if one does, it will tempt you to look for another, and you'll likely lose it all. Sometimes the best investments are the ones we don't make.
- **Invest in what you understand.** If you don't have expertise in an area, seek a professional's opinion. Before hiring a financial advisor, do your homework. Always check references. Some financial advisors charge fees, others make commissions, and some work with a combination of the two. It may be best to hire a financial advisor who charges an hourly fee or a set fee so that they are motivated to put your investment in the best

instrument, not the one that makes them the biggest commission.

- **Never borrow money to invest.** If your investment does not work, you are stuck with the debt to repay.
- **Create memories.** If you are the head of the finances in your family and you are one of the 10 percent in society who is incredibly frugal, be sure to spend some money creating memories with your family. Taking vacations, buying gifts, and celebrating special days and achievements can help accomplish this.

If you practice sound financial principles with what you have today, then regardless of your current financial state, your finances will gradually grow and you'll be able to manage whatever finances come your way.

Please answer all of the following questions independently of your spouse. Do not compare answers until our next session. However, work together with your spouse to complete the budget and financial statement.

1. **On a scale of 1 to 10 (10 being best), how good is your ability to manage money?**

2. **Which one of you pays the bills? Why?**

3. **Fill in the blank. I think any *discretionary* purchase over the following amount should require the agreement of both the husband and the wife:**

   $_____

---

4. Identify an area where your spouse spends money which you don't understand the value or importance of.

5. If you received a sweepstakes cash award of $50,000, what would you recommend you do with it as a couple?

6. What do you believe your current FICO score is?

7. What is your biggest concern regarding your finances?

8. Complete an Annual Budget and a Financial Statement of Net Worth together *with* your spouse. You can use the guides on the following pages to assist you.

Annual Budget

- To figure out the percentage, divide the annual amount of the expense by your annual net income.
- Your annual total budget must match your annual net income.
- Your annual net income is your gross income minus all payroll deductions.
- If you have more income than you have expenses, add the additional amount to savings to balance your budget.

Use line 14 for anything not covered in 1 through 13.

	Category	Percentage	Annual Amount
1.	Giving to God	%	$
2.	Housing (mortgage or rent)	%	$
3.	Food	%	$
4.	Car payment(s)	%	$
5.	Insurance (home, car, health, life, etc.)	%	$
6.	Debt	%	$
7.	Medical/dental	%	$
8.	Clothing	%	$
9.	Savings	%	$
10.	Entertainment/recreation	%	$
11.	Utilities	%	$
12.	Cell phones	%	$
13.	Cable bill	%	$
14.	Other	%	$
	Total*	100%	$

* Must equal your annual net income.

Financial Statement of Net Worth

Complete the Financial Statement of Net Worth with your spouse.

Assets		Amount
1.	Cash (savings, checking, money market, etc.)	
2.	Stocks, mutual funds, bonds	
3.	Partnerships	
4.	Home (current market value)	
5.	Other real estate (current market value)	
6.	Notes and Deeds of Trust (for which you are the beneficiary)	
7.	Retirement account	
8.	Furnishings (estimate cash value)	
9.	Automobile (current low Blue Book)	
10.	Collections	
11.	Miscellaneous (any other assets)	
12.	**Total value of assets (sum)**	

Liabilities		Amount
13.	Mortgage (current payoff)	
14.	Automobile loans	
15.	Credit card debt	
16.	Other loans	
17.	Outstanding bills	
18.	Misc. (any other liabilities)	
19.	**Total liabilities (sum)**	

Totals		Amount
20.	Total assets (from 12 above)	
21.	Total liabilities (from 19 above)	
22.	**Net worth (difference)**	

CHAPTER 17

Marriage Goals

Commit to the LORD whatever you do, and your
plans will succeed—Proverbs 16:3

ONE OF OUR (ED'S AND ANGIE'S) favorite family vacation spots is the lake. We especially enjoy watching sailboats serenely gliding along the water. When a boat sails from one port to another, it doesn't sail in a straight line. As the winds shift, the captain constantly tacks back and forth, correcting his direction to stay on course.

A marriage requires the same type of navigation. To think that you will always be on course is unrealistic. That is why it is important to intentionally and thoughtfully steer your marriage in the direction you want it to go.

Over time marriages get better or get worse. They don't stay the same. By participating in this marriage enrichment program, you've chosen to navigate your marriage on a course that will make it stronger. We want to finish by helping you put into place a strategy for continuing to nurture and grow your marriage in the oneness with which God wants to bless you. "In his heart a man plans his course, but the LORD determines his steps" (Proverbs 16:9).

An important step towards navigating well in marriage is setting goals that please God. So let's look at some basic steps for setting successful goals and establishing future plans for your marriage that will please the Lord.

1. **Brainstorm the goals you want to set.** When setting goals for your marriage, come together as a couple. Both of you should have a say in the goals. If only one

of you makes the goals, it will be like one hand clapping. You want to operate as a team. Be willing to compromise in order to find agreement on the goals you set. After you have discussed all possible goals, decide on a few positive goals that you can both be excited about achieving.

2. **Pray for God's guidance in your goals.** Proverbs 3:5–6 says, "Trust in the LORD with all your heart and lean not on your own understanding; in all your ways acknowledge him, and he will make your paths straight." How foolish that we try to journey through life in our own will when God promises, "'For I know the plans I have for you,' declares the LORD, 'plans to prosper you and not to harm you, plans to give you hope and a future'" (Jeremiah 29:11). We may not know what our future holds, but we know who holds our future: GOD! And He has great plans for us! Consult with Him.

3. **Write down your goals.** Be specific when writing down your goals and set a timeline for accomplishing them. Research shows that those who write down their goals accomplish significantly more than those who do not write out their goals.[20] Writing down goals clarifies thinking and makes our goals more real.

4. **Create action steps for each goal, and set a specific time to put your steps into action.** To simply write a goal down and believe we will achieve it is usually not enough. Action steps along the way will help you make progress on your goals. For example, if your goal is to join a small group, you might make the following action steps: (1) Contact the church to find out what small groups are available; (2) set a time and place you and your spouse will discuss the best small group for you; and (3) set a date that you will call the small group leader to express your interest in joining the group. Remember, the way we live our days is the way we live our lives. If we live our days without intentionally

An important step towards navigating well in marriage is setting goals that please God

---

[20] Sid Savara, "Writing Down Your Goals—The Harvard Written Goal Study. Fact or Fiction?" Personal Development Training with Sid Savara, http://sidsavara.com/personal-productivity/fact-or-fiction-the-truth-about-the-harvard-written-goal-study (accessed July 4, 2012).

taking action, our lives will reflect the inaction and we will not make progress towards our goals.

Action steps are simply small goals on the way to a larger goal. When Sea World wanted to teach Shamu the whale to jump over a bar placed thirty feet above the water, the trainers started by having Shamu simply swim over a rope at the bottom of the pool. They rewarded him each time he did this correctly. They then raised the rope a few feet at a time until Shamu could jump over the bar thirty feet above the pool. They achieved their big goal by taking smaller action steps along the way. Taking small steps daily will help us realize our goals too.

5. **Review your goals.** Set a time to periodically review your goals to make sure that you are on track. At that point, you can either celebrate achieving your designated action steps or make the needed adjustments.

There are many goals you and your spouse may want to set in your marriage. Below are just a few categories you may want to consider for establishing goals.

Spiritual goals. The foundational spiritual goal should be to always keep Christ at the center of your marriage. It may be manifested by joining a small group at church, committing to attend church each week, selecting a ministry, setting a regular time to pray as a couple, setting a regular time to read the Bible, etc. If you want to see God's Word become more real in your life, think of a personal trait you wish to improve. Find a verse in the Bible that reflects the change you wish to make in this area. For example, if you often dominate conversations, you might select James 1:19: "Everyone should be quick to listen, slow to speak and slow to become angry." Focus on the verse you choose for a year and watch how God works in your life. Just imagine: after ten years of doing this, you will have improved ten of your weakest traits.

Time commitment to each other. Make a goal to spend some special time on a regular basis with your spouse. This might be committing to walking together three times a week, establishing a weekly date night, or taking a class together at a community college. Before all the busyness of the world closes in on you, schedule special time together.

Family goals. Although this program focuses on your relationship as husband and wife, if you have additional family members in your household, set some shared family goals too. You may want to have a family game night or movie night. Or set date nights with individual kids. Perhaps you can challenge your kids to choose a Bible verse to memorize and live by for the year. The better you operate as a team in front of your kids, the healthier relationship you will model to them. The greatest gift you can give your kids is to love your spouse.

Vacation plans. Sometimes financial strains on your budget limit the vacation fund, but this should not eliminate spending some fun vacation time at least once a year. The point is not how expensive a vacation you take, but rather that you take a vacation. You can do something as simple as spend a week at home having an itinerary each day of doing something fun together. There are many things you can do together that cost little or nothing: spend a day at the beach, go on a picnic, go hiking, camp in your own backyard, etc. Use your imagination and be original. Create memories!

Goals for yourself. Have a goal for something for yourself. Your marriage vow of becoming one does not mean you cannot have individual goals as well. You may want to take a dance class, join a softball league, take up a hobby, start a book club, or learn a new skill. By continuing to grow in new ways, you will remain fresh and interesting to your spouse. Encourage your spouse to set personal goals too.

Financial goals. We covered financial goals in detail in the last chapter. Be sure to review these goals every year or whenever your finances change significantly. Remember, https://wwws.mint.com is a free resource that can assist you with setting and evaluating your financial goals.

Health and fitness goals. You will both enjoy each other and life more if you are healthy and fit. Set goals to help

There is nothing more important to your career than having a joyful marriage

maintain your health. Be supportive of one another in this area, not critical.

You might notice we didn't list professional goals. Professional goals are important too, but make sure they leave room for giving the right attention to your marriage. Research has shown that when marriage is kept in its rightful place in your priorities, it will benefit you in every other layer of your life.[21] There is nothing more important to your career than having a joyful marriage.

We were recently in a coffee shop and overheard an older man at a nearby table say to his wife with a chuckle, "If I had nown I was going to live this long, I would have taken better care of myself." Looking back on your life with regrets is no fun. Hindsight gives clarity and insight. There are many ways we could complete the man's statement, "If I had known _____, I would have _____." It is our prayer that you will put so much foresight into your marriage and will be so guided by God's hand that you will look back on your life with fulfillment and joy.

Please answer the following questions independently of your spouse. Do not compare your answers until our next session.

1. **What Bible verse would you like to commit to memory this year? This verse should focus on helping you improve one area in your life.**

---

[21] Tyler Ward. "3 Things I Wish I Knew Before We God Married." http://www.tylerwardis.com/3-things-i-wish-i-knew-before-we-got-married/#more-794 (accessed December 8, 2014).

2. List some of your ideas for goals in the following areas:

Type of Goal	Goal Ideas
Spiritual	
Time with each other	
Family	
Vacation	
Personal	
Health and fitness	

3. Make a date with your spouse to develop goals as a
    couple. Write below the specific date, time, and
    place you agree to meet.

CHAPTER 18

Keeping the Flame Going

The fear of the LORD is the beginning of wisdom,
and knowledge of the Holy One is understanding
—Proverbs 9:10

TURN BACK TO PAGE 5 AND read your answer to question 2 (chapter 1). How well did you achieve what you were hoping to accomplish through this program?

The purpose of this Marriage Enrichment Program is to reveal God's blueprint for marriage. The intent was not to build the house for you, but to give you the tools and the materials to build your home following God's blueprint.

Knowledge fades with time unless you refresh what you have learned. This chapter is designed to provide a resource so that you can periodically review what you have learned and give your marriage a tune-up.

Here is how it works. Set a time at least quarterly to review the twenty-one questions below with your spouse. Hopefully you will be able to answer positively to most of the questions. However, some of your responses will likely reveal that your marriage needs some improvement in those areas. Each question will be followed with some encouragement on that topic and will direct you to the chapter in your workbook where you can go to refresh that area of your marriage.

Read all twenty-one questions before answering the two homework questions that are at the end of this chapter.

1. **Are all three types of love (eros, philia, and agape) present in your marriage?**

Review the list you wrote of ten things you love about your spouse. Discuss together how you can each express the three types of love towards each other more fully. Keep this list available and refer to it often. Whenever you become discouraged about your marriage, re-read the list of things you love about your spouse. One of the most effective tools for overcoming marital disappointment is replacing a negative thought about your husband or wife with thoughts of gratitude. Studies show that we can focus on only one emotion at a time: choose love. (Refer to chapter 2.)

2. **Have you both forgiven each other for everything?**

Make sure forgiveness flows freely between you and your spouse for conflicts both BIG and small. Practice forgiving, not collecting, hurts. God has forgiven us for all of our sins. He wants us to forgive one another freely. "Bear with each other and forgive whatever grievances you may have against one another. Forgive as the Lord forgave you" (Colossians 3:13). We forgive by faith, out of obedience to God. God wants us to love others and to love Him. This love He speaks of is a choice, not a feeling. We must trust God to complete His work in us. Make it between you and God and not between you and your spouse. Turn your heart over to God. Corrie ten Boom, a Christian who survived a Nazi concentration camp, said, "Forgiveness is the key that unlocks the door of resentment and the handcuffs of hatred. It is a power that breaks the chains of bitterness and the shackles of selfishness."[22] One of the most loving actions you can continually take is forgiving. (Refer to chapter 3.)

3. **Are you living out the biblical roles outlined for a husband and wife in Ephesians 5:21–33?**

We each need to worshipfully surrender our lives to Christ. Ultimately, a wife answers to God for how well

---

[22] Corrie ten Boom, *Clippings from My Notebook*, (Nashville: Thomas Nelson, 1982), 19.

she submits to her husband's leadership, whether or not he is making good, loving decisions. Ultimately, a husband answers to God for how well he loves his wife, regardless of whether or not she respects and submits to him.

When your spouse falls short of living out God's will in your marriage, take your frustrations to God. Trust God to meet your needs, and he will fill you with his love to take back into the marriage. In doing this, instead of expecting perfect behavior from two imperfect people, you look for the perfect response from your perfect God. (Refer to chapter 4.)

4. Are you continuing to pray together often?

If not, set a time at least once a week to pray together. Remember, God wants to bless your marriage beyond your imagination, but you need to invite Him in and follow His will together. There is nothing more important than keeping God at the center of your marriage. (Refer to chapter 4.)

5. Do you continue to share specifically with your spouse how he or she can pray for you?

Prayer is one of the most loving, intimate expressions that can be exchanged between a husband and wife. After you share your prayer requests with each other, pray out loud together for each other. (Refer to chapter 4.)

6. Is your spouse meeting your most important wants and needs?

You may desire a weekly date night; time to talk about light topics; fun together doing a hobby; more frequent sex; more transparency with the finances; more home cooking; staying physically fit; entertaining more with family and friends; hearing more affirming statements; having more intimate, open, honest conversations; etc. Share your desires in a loving way with your spouse.

We should not look to our spouse to make us happy. There will be times in your marriage when it will be more profitable to take the focus off of your partner meeting your wants and onto God. Philippians

4:19 assures us, "God will meet all your needs according to his glorious riches in Christ Jesus." Bob and Judy Hughes' book, *Love Focused,* is an excellent resource to understand this concept better. They also have a couples Bible study you could do together. (Refer to chapter 5.)

7. Have you established a weekly King for the Day and Queen for the Day?

Share with each other what you would like for your spouse to do for you on your day. Be attentive to meeting your spouse's wishes on his or her day. Remember, this can be a real game-changer! (Refer to chapter 5.)

8. Are there any areas in which you feel your spouse is not successfully fulfilling his or her role in marriage?

God gives specific instructions for husbands to love their wives as Christ loved the church. God instructs wives to respect their husbands and submit to their leadership in the family. Lovingly discuss any areas you would like to see improved, and share what betterment looks like. (Refer to chapter 5.)

9. Are you spending most of your time in the sweet spot?

A marriage has momentum in the direction of the sweet spot or the sour patch. If you are not spending the majority of your time in the sweet spot, go back and review the eighteen skills for staying in the sweet spot. Remember, fun is the litmus test of a good relationship. Do something fun together. (Refer to chapter 6.)

10. Are you dealing effectively with your incompatibilities?

A great marriage is not based on marrying someone compatible, because God does not make any two people perfectly compatible; it is based on learning how to deal effectively with your incompatibilities. Try making this your mantra. If you are struggling with compatibility, consider taking a Myers-Briggs Type

Indicator® instrument to identify your personality styles (http://www.16personalities.com offers a free test online). Remember there is not a right or wrong to personality differences. You are both created in the image of God. Work on becoming more understanding and accepting of the fact that you approach life differently. (Refer to chapter 7.)

11. Are the differences between men and women causing friction in your marriage?

Men and women have very different operating systems. We will never completely understand each other, but we can educate ourselves on what is important to each other. God wants our differences to complement and complete each other in marriage as we work together as one. (Refer to chapter 8.)

12. On a scale of 1 to 10, how full is your love tank? What can your spouse do to make it a 10?

Remember to speak to your spouse in his or her love language, and remind your spouse to talk to you in your language. You may want to read the book, *The Five Love Languages*, by Gary Chapman. (Refer to chapter 9.)

13. Are there any issues with your family relationships that are causing problems in your marriage?

Discuss what you can do to improve any family tension. Be sure that your relationship with each other is kept primary and that you always show a united front. When problems arise with your family, face them together. Discuss them together as husband and wife. Pray about them together. If needed, seek outside counsel from trusted advisors or professionals. Finally, keep things in perspective. Don't major in minors. If it is not going to be life altering for your child, natural consequences may be the best teacher. If extended family members are causing issues, sometimes it is best to set healthy boundaries to protect your primary family relationships. (Refer to chapter 10.)

14. Are you communicating with each other effectively?

Content, tone, and body language are all important aspects of communication, but listening and choosing the appropriate time for sensitive conversations are also important. Work on any weaknesses in your communication. When couples are having trouble with communication, it is often a symptom of a bigger issue. Try to identify the bigger issue and work that through with the other tools offered through this program (such as the "Ten Rules to Resolve Conflict" in appendix 8). Above all, always speak to each other in love using the rules for discussion. (Refer to chapter 11.)

15. Do you have any unresolved conflict in your marriage?

Conflicts come in all shapes and sizes. With moderate conflicts, use the Start or Stop and Continue Method. If you have a major conflict, set a time to use the "Ten Rules to Resolve Conflict" in appendix 8 to resolve your conflict. (Refer to chapter 12.)

16. Are you enjoying the emotional intimacy you desire with your spouse?

You should feel comfortable and safe sharing your most intimate thoughts and dreams with each other. It is as if you are saying, "into-me-see." Growing in this area involves a continual effort and investment in your relationship. (Refer to chapter 13.)

17. Do you have a vibrant sex life?

If your love life isn't all that you would like it to be, the best way to revitalize your physical intimacy is to communicate openly and honestly with each other. Truthfully communicate your desires to your spouse. Be sensitive and loving in fulfilling your partner's wishes. Try something fun like showering together. (Refer to chapter 14.)

18. Is your marriage safely affair-proofed?

It's too late to prevent an affair after it's happened. Protect your marriage by keeping proper boundaries in place. Discuss if there are any areas that need to be reinforced. (Refer to chapter 15.)

19. Are your finances healthy?

Be transparent with each other with your spending. Recognize that you will likely have different ways you will each want to spend discretionary income. Provided it fits into your budget, be understanding of your differences. A budget and financial statement are good ways to keep on track with your finances. A helpful tool for creating a budget and maintaining transparency with your finances is https://www.mint.com. If you need some extra guidance on your finances, many churches offer financial counseling following either Dave Ramsey's principles or Crown Ministries. Find information on these programs at www.daveramsey.com and www.crown.org. (Refer to chapter 16.)

20. Have you set goals together as a couple?

One of the cornerstones to this program is having an intentional marriage. Relationships are either getting better or getting worse. They don't stay the same. It is important to continue pursuing goals and dreams as a couple. In order for this to happen you need to set goals and take action steps. In order for goals to truly take hold they should be written down and reviewed for progress. (Refer to Chapter 17.)

21. Are you involved in a small group for couples?

Fellowship with other believers is one of the conduits God uses to share His truth with us. Communing with other Christian married couples will help enrich your marriage through shared life experiences and godly insights. (Refer to chapter 17.)

In most cases, these steps will be enough to put your marriage back on track. In some cases, you may need additional help. If you feel that your relationship may need additional help, talk with your pastor or a professional counselor for guidance. Your marriage is important. Take the proper steps to ensure that you experience God's best.

Have you ever noticed that the Bible begins and ends with a marriage? It begins with the coming together of Adam and Eve: "For this reason a man will leave his father and mother and be united to his wife, and they will become one flesh" (Genesis 2:24). It ends with believers being joined with Christ in marriage at the wedding supper of the Lamb (Revelation 19). The marriage relationship is a picture of the relationship God desires to have with each of us. God did not intend to have a distant relationship with people. He created us to have a loving relationship with Him now and for all eternity. By keeping a Christ-focus in your marriage during both the good times and the struggles, you will know what it means to put the "happily" in your ever after!

Please answer the following question independently of your spouse. Do not compare your answer until our next session.

1. **In taking inventory on your marriage today using the questions above, which areas did you identify as still needing growth? Be honest. Please list the numbers of those questions.**

2. **Put a date on your calendar for your next quarterly marriage assessment and tune-up. Write the date below.**

Appendices

Appendix 1 ❧ What it Means to be a Submissive Wife

Appendix 2 ❧ What it Means to be a Godly Husband

Appendix 3 ❧ Guide to Planning a Date Night with Your Spouse

Appendix 4 ❧ The Five Love Languages Test for Wives

Appendix 5 ❧ The Five Love Languages Test for Husbands

Appendix 6 ❧ Love Languages Guide

Appendix 7 ❧ Rules for Discussion

Appendix 8 ❧ Ten Rules to Resolve Conflict

Appendix 9 ❧ Ten Ways to be a Fantastic Wife

Appendix 10 ❧ Ten Ways to be a Fantastic Husband

What it Means to be a
Submissive Wife

ↂ

ULTIMATELY, WHEN A WIFE submits to her husband she is doing it out of obedience to God. Jesus (who is co-equal to and co-eternal with God the Father and the Holy Spirit) modeled submission to us by perfectly doing the will of God the Father in everything He said and did on earth. A wife should follow this example by worshipfully surrendering her life to Christ by:

- Following her husband's leadership
- Respecting and trusting her husband's opinion
- Seeking her husband's counsel when making decisions
- Believing in her husband's ability to succeed in his areas of responsibility
- Being her husband's helpmate
- Honoring her husband by talking about him in a positive way
- Praising, affirming, and appreciating her husband
- Being a team player
- Being her husband's #1 fan!
- Serving her husband with sacrificial love
- Avoiding non-biblical criticism or nagging
- Not comparing him unfavorably to others
- Not blaming or controlling him
- Not correcting him in front of others

A wife will ultimately answer to God for how well she submits to her husband's leadership whether or not he is making good, loving decisions. However, a wife should not follow her husband into sinful behavior, for God is her ultimate authority.

When a wife is not happy with the direction her husband is leading she should take her frustrations to God with an open teachable spirit. God may be doing a work inside of her through her obedience to submit. God may be protecting her through the direction her husband is leading over what she feels is best. God may want her to lovingly share her thoughts with her husband on why they should follow a different path. God may want to work on her husband's heart while she submits her desires to the Lord. God does not need her to be the Holy Spirit, or a "holy nag." God wants her to trust Him to meet her needs and give her the proper response.

God ultimately wants you to operate together as one with your husband. Pray for God to either change your husband's mind or change your heart. In doing this, instead of requiring perfect behavior from two imperfect people, you are looking for the perfect protection and guidance from our perfect God.

What it Means to be a Godly Husband

ભ

- **Individual scheduled prayer.** I (Ed) pray each morning in the shower. I pick shower time because it is something I do every day. It does not matter when you pray; it only matters that you are consistent with it.

- **Individual random prayer.** Pray for the events of the day. For example, I often pray before meetings, mentoring sessions, and time with friends or family. Angie and I often silently pray for our couples during our mentoring sessions.

- **Couple/family scheduled prayer.** Have a set time at least once a week for a prayer session. Angie and I meet twenty minutes before we would normally leave for church each week to pray as a couple. Many couples pray together more often. Some couples pray in bed together every day. Praying with and for your wife at the end of the day can be some of the best foreplay.

- **Couple/family random prayer.** Pray as a couple for special events and situations. Remember, prayer can be anywhere even in a car or an elevator.

- **Attend church.** Many Christians will attend church when it is convenient. Make attending church as a family a priority.

- **Spend time in God's word.** This is a way God can talk to us, and a relationship requires two way communication. The more of the Bible we comprehend, the better we are prepared to deal with the world.

- **Give your time, talents, and treasures to God.** A great way to give your time and talents is to get involved in a ministry. When Angie and I got involved in the premarital counseling program at church, we did it to give back to God. Little did we know that God was going to pour out blessing on us. Remember, your first ministry is to your wife and kids. In Malachi 3:10 God ask us to test Him in our giving. He promises to open the floodgates of heaven and pour out so much blessing that there will not be room enough to store it.

- **Make godly decisions.** Big decisions require God at the center. Pray about it, see what the Bible has to say about it, listen carefully to what your wife has to say about it, seek the counsel of Christian mentors, and then make your decision.

- **Love your wife selflessly.** Husbands are instructed to sacrificially love their wives using Jesus as their example. This means doing what is most loving even if it is not what is easiest or what you want for yourself.

> Husbands, love your wives, just as Christ loved the church and gave himself up for her…. In this same way, husbands ought to love their wives as their own bodies. He who loves his wife loves himself. After all, no one ever hated his own body, but he feeds and cares for it, just as Christ does the church—for we are members of his body.
>
> —Ephesians 5:25, 28-30

- **Love God.** God's greatest commandment is to love God with all your heart, soul, mind, and strength.
- **Love others.** God's second greatest commandment it to love others.

APPENDIX 3

Guide to Planning a Date Night with Your Spouse

❧

EITHER SPOUSE CAN PLAN A date night. The date night could be an evening out or a romantic night in. Here are some tips to help make it a special event.

- **Plan your date.** Create anticipation by setting your date a few days off. Show your devotion to your spouse by putting some effort into your planning. It doesn't need to cost a lot of money, but planning ahead and taking care of any details shows your thoughtfulness. Try to keep in mind things that your spouse would enjoy. If at any time things don't go perfectly during the date, view it as an adventure and laugh about it. The most important thing is that the two of you are together.

- **Set the mood in the morning.** Write a fun message to your spouse on the bathroom mirror with an erasable marker. I (Ed) recently wrote to Angie, "Out of 7 billion people in the world, God blessed me with the best wife of all!"

- **Build anticipation.** Text or call your spouse during the day to say how much you look forward to your date.

- **Set the tone.** If you are going out, get your car cleaned. Put a nice air freshener in the car. Have some music to play that you both enjoy. If you are staying in, light some scented candles. Create the appropriate environment for your activity.

APPENDIX 4

The Five Love Languages Test for Wives

ॐ

Circle the letter that corresponds to the answer that most accurately describes how you feel. Circle only one letter in each numbered set of questions.[23]

1.	Sweet notes from my husband make me feel good.	A
	I love my husband's hugs.	E
2.	I like to be alone with my husband.	B
	I feel loved when my husband washes my car.	D
3.	Receiving special gifts from my husband makes me happy.	C
	I enjoy long trips with my husband.	B
4.	I feel loved when my husband helps me with the laundry.	D
	I like it when my husband touches me.	E
5.	I feel loved when my husband puts his arm around me.	E
	I know my husband loves me because he surprises me with gifts.	C
6.	I like going most anywhere with my husband.	B
	I like to hold my husband's hand.	E
7.	I value the gifts my husband gives me.	C
	I love to hear my husband say he loves me.	A

---

[23] Gary Chapman, "Love Languages Personal Profiles: For Wives," The 5 Love Languages®, http://www.5lovelanguages.com/assessments/love/ (accessed June 27, 2012).

8.	I like for my husband to sit close to me.	E
	My husband tells me I look good, and I like that.	A
9.	Spending time with my husband makes me happy.	B
	Even the smallest gift from my husband is important to me.	C
10.	I feel loved when my husband tells me he is proud of me.	A
	When my husband helps clean up after me, I know that he loves me.	D
11.	No matter what we do, I love doing things with my husband.	B
	Supportive comments from my husband make me feel good.	A
12.	Little things my husband does for me mean more to me than things he says.	D
	I love to hug my husband.	E
13.	My husband's praise means a lot to me.	A
	It means a lot to me that my husband gives me gifts I really like.	C
14.	Just being around my husband makes me feel good.	B
	I love it when my husband gives me a massage.	E
15.	My husband's reactions to my accomplishments are so encouraging.	A
	It means a lot to me when my husband helps with something I know he hates.	D
16.	I never get tired of my husband's kisses.	E
	I love that my husband shows real interest in the things I like to do.	B

17.	I can count on my husband to help me with projects.	D
	I still get excited when opening a gift from my husband.	C
18.	I love for my husband to compliment my appearance.	A
	I love that my husband listens to me and respects my ideas.	B
19.	I can't help but touch my husband when he's close by.	E
	My husband sometimes runs errands for me, and I appreciate that.	D
20.	My husband deserves an award for all the things he does to help me.	D
	I'm sometimes amazed at how thoughtful my husband's gifts to me are.	C
21.	I love having my husband's undivided attention.	B
	I love that my husband helps clean the house.	D
22.	I look forward to seeing what my husband gives me for my birthday.	C
	I never get tired of hearing my husband tell me that I am important to him.	A
23.	My husband lets me know he loves me by giving me gifts.	C
	My husband shows his love by helping me without me having to ask.	D
24.	My husband doesn't interrupt me when I am talking, and I like that.	B
	I never get tired of receiving gifts from my husband.	C
25.	My husband is good about asking how he can help when I'm tired.	D
	It doesn't matter where we go, I just like going places with my husband.	B

26.	I love cuddling with my husband.	E
	I love surprise gifts from my husband.	C
27.	My husband's encouraging words give me confidence.	A
	I love to watch movies with my husband.	B
28.	I couldn't ask for any better gifts than the ones my husband gives me.	C
	I love it that my husband can't keep his hands off me.	E
29.	It means a lot to me when my husband helps me despite being busy.	D
	It makes me feel really good when my husband tells me he appreciates me.	A
30.	I love hugging and kissing my husband after we've been apart for a while.	E
	I love hearing my husband tell me that he believes in me.	A

APPENDIX 5

The Five Love Languages Test for Husbands

∾

Circle the letter that corresponds to the answer that most accurately describes how you feel. Circle only one letter in each numbered set of questions.[24]

1.	My wife's love notes make me feel good.	A
	I love my wife's hugs.	E
2.	I like to be alone with my wife.	B
	I feel loved when my wife helps me do yard work.	D
3.	Receiving special gifts from my wife makes me happy.	C
	I enjoy long trips with my wife.	B
4.	I feel loved when my wife does my laundry.	D
	I like it when my wife touches me.	E
5.	I feel loved when my wife puts her arm around me.	E
	I know my wife loves me because she surprises me with gifts.	C

---

[24] Gary Chapman, "Love Languages Personal Profiles: For Husbands," The 5 Love Languages®, http://www.5lovelanguages.com/assessments/love/ (accessed June 27, 2012).

6.	I like going most anywhere with my wife.	B
	I like to hold my wife's hand.	E
7.	I value the gifts my wife gives me.	C
	I love to hear my wife say she loves me.	A
8.	I like for my wife to sit close to me.	E
	My wife tells me I look good, and I like that.	A
9.	Spending time with my wife makes me happy.	B
	Even the smallest gift from my wife is important to me.	C
10.	I feel loved when my wife tells me she is proud of me.	A
	When my wife cooks a meal for me, I know that she loves me.	D
11.	No matter what we do, I love doing things with my wife.	B
	Supportive comments from my wife make me feel good.	A
12.	Little things my wife does for me mean more to me than things she says.	D
	I love to hug my wife.	E
13.	My wife's praise means a lot to me.	A
	It means a lot to me that my wife gives me gifts I really like.	C
14.	Just being around my wife makes me feel good.	B
	I love it when my wife gives me a back rub.	E
15.	My wife's reactions to my accomplishments are so encouraging.	A
	It means a lot to me when my wife helps with something I know she hates.	D
16.	I never get tired of my wife's kisses.	E
	I love that my wife shows real interest in the things I like to do.	B

17.	I can count on my wife to help me with projects.	D
	I still get excited when opening a gift from my wife.	C
18.	I love for my wife to compliment my appearance.	A
	I love that my wife listens to me and respects my ideas.	B
19.	I can't help but touch my wife when she's close by.	E
	My wife sometimes runs errands for me, and I appreciate that.	D
20.	My wife deserves an award for all the things she does to help me.	D
	I'm sometimes amazed at how thoughtful my wife's gifts to me are.	C
21.	I love having my wife's undivided attention.	B
	Keeping the house clean is an important act of service.	D
22.	I look forward to seeing what my wife gives me for my birthday.	C
	I never get tired of hearing my wife tell me that I am important to her.	A
23.	My wife lets me know she loves me by giving me gifts.	C
	My wife shows her love by helping me catch up on projects around the house.	D
24.	My wife doesn't interrupt me when I am talking, and I like that.	B
	I never get tired of receiving gifts from my wife.	C
25.	My wife can tell when I'm tired and she's good about asking how she can help.	D
	It doesn't matter where we go, I just like going places with my wife.	B

26.	I love having sex with my wife.	E
	I love surprise gifts from my wife.	C
27.	My wife's encouraging words give me confidence.	A
	I love to watch movies with my wife.	B
28.	I couldn't ask for any better gifts than the ones my wife gives me.	C
	I just can't keep my hands off my wife.	E
29.	It means a lot to me when my wife helps me despite having other things to do.	D
	It makes me feel really good when my wife tells me she appreciates me.	A
30.	I love hugging and kissing my wife after we've been apart for a while.	E
	I love hearing my wife tell me that she believes in me.	A

APPENDIX 6

Love Languages Guide

Love Language	Actions	Avoid
Words of Affirmation	• Compliments • Notes and cards • Kind words	Criticism
Quality Time	• One-to-one time • Face-to-face interaction • Taking long walks together • Doing things together	Interrupting special time together
Receiving Gifts	• Giving gifts on special and not-so-special days • More about the thoughtfulness of the gift than the expense of the gift	Ignoring special days
Acts of Service	• Helping with chores • Saying things like, "How can I help you?"	Helping others and not being there for your spouse
Physical Touch	• Touches • Hugs & cuddling • Kisses	Negative touch

Chart based on Gary Chapman's book, *The Five Love Languages.*

APPENDIX 7

Rules for Discussion

ↀ

1. Speak in a quiet voice.
2. Do not interrupt.
3. Do not bring up the past.
4. Do not blame.
5. Do not use profanity.
6. Do not criticize.
7. Use "I feel" statements, not attacking "you" statements.
8. State *your* feelings, not your spouse's.
9. Never threaten your relationship.

APPENDIX 8

Ten Rules to Resolve Conflict

∾

1. Define the issue to be resolved.
2. Set a time to meet.
3. Set a private place to meet.
4. Begin in prayer.
5. Each share your position.
6. Each point out what he or she has done to contribute to the problem.
7. Each point out what he or she can do to help resolve the issue.
8. Agree on a resolution acceptable to both.
9. Write down the resolution.
10. End in prayer.

Ten Ways to be a Fantastic Wife

1. Believe in your husband and be his number one fan.
2. Be careful not to nag your husband. Turn over your concerns to God in prayer. Ask God to give you oneness in your marriage.
3. It is not uncommon for a husband to have a greater sex drive than his wife. Take care of his sexual needs.
4. On the first day of each month, put the following question on your calendar: "What must it be like to be married to me?"
5. People tend to be what you say they are. Tell your husband what a great husband, friend, and lover he is. He won't disappoint you.
6. When you come together at the end of the day, greet each other in a loving way.
7. Guys are visual; do your best to take care of yourself and be attractive to him.
8. Remember to speak in his love language.
9. Share in his hobbies with him. Continue to be the fun person he married.
10. Put Christ at the center of your life and at the center of your marriage.

APPENDIX 10

Ten Ways to be a Fantastic Husband

✂

1. Always show your wife how special she is to you.
2. Avoid being too critical. What you may think of as constructive criticism, she may see as an attack on her.
3. If you want to have a great sex life, you must keep some romance in your relationship. Continue to date your wife!
4. On the first day of each month, put the following question on your calendar: "What must it be like to be married to me?"
5. Write down your wife's anniversary, her birthday, and Valentine's Day, and put them on your calendar. Log yourself a reminder for each December 31 to add these dates to the next year's calendar.
6. Compliment your wife's appearance. She knows you are visual. Your compliments are important to her.
7. People tend to be what you say they are. Tell your wife what a great wife, friend, and lover she is. She won't disappoint you.
8. Remember to talk in her love language.
9. Your wife will need to talk. Take time to be a good listener. Often, she won't want a solution; she just wants to talk to you. Value her opinion.
10. Put Christ at the center of your life and marriage, and be the spiritual leader of your family.

Acknowledgement

A big thank you to Jean E Jones. You embraced our vision with care as you gave heartfelt attention to every detail in critiquing, editing, and formatting our materials.

CPSIA information can be obtained
at www.ICGtesting.com
Printed in the USA
LVOW03s1940241116
514292LV00027B/529/P